The ART® of Trading

Combining the Science of Technical Analysis with the Art of Reality-Based Trading®

BENNETT A. McDOWELL

WILEY

John Wiley & Sons, Inc.

Published by John Wiley & Sons, Inc., Hoboken, New Jersey.
Published simultaneously in Canada.

For general information on our other products and services or for technical support, please contact our Customer Care Department within the United States at (800) 762-2974, outside the United States at (317) 572-3993 or fax (317) 572-4002.

Wiley also publishes its books in a variety of electronic formats. Some content that appears in print may not be available in electronic formats. For more information about Wiley products, visit our Web site at www.wiley.com.

Designations used by companies to distinguish their products are often claimed as trademarks. In all instances where John Wiley & Sons, Inc. is aware of a claim, the product names appear in initial capital or all capital letters. Readers, however, should contact the appropriate companies for more complete information regarding trademarks and registration.

Library of Congress Cataloging-in-Publication Data:

McDowell, Bennett, 1957–
The art of trading: combining the science of technical analysis with the art of reality based trading / Bennett McDowell.
    p.   cm. – (Wiley trading series)
    Includes index.
    ISBN 978-0-470-18772-2 (cloth/dvd)
    1. Investment analysis.   2. Speculation.   3. Stocks.
    I. Title.

    HG4529.M385   2008
    332.63'2042–dc22

                        2007049357

Printed in the United States of America.

10 9 8 7 6 5 4 3 2 1

For my children, Heather Frances and Brady Bennett,
with love and affection.

Contents

Foreword

This is not your ordinary "get rich quick" book about trading the stock market. Rather, it is a guide to a multimedia approach to learning and trading, using the Applied Reality Trading® (ART®) method of trading. This book and the accompanying DVD explain the concepts and methodology. In addition, the purchase of this book includes a one-month time frame in which to actually learn to trade the system and apply it in real time. This is done by including the ART software for one month, including access to live streaming data and access to a few, designated brokerage firms that can trade directly through the software. In essence, everything that the reader needs—for learning and for seeing how the system works in actual markets—is included with this book.

The ART trading methodology is built on software recognition of several time-tested patterns that can be easily identified for the user. While they are called specific names in the software, these are essentially breakouts and reversals—the meat and potatoes of technical trading. The chart patterns identified can be applied to any type of bar chart—daily, five-minute, weekly, and so on. Moreover, they can be applied to stocks, futures, indices, and forex—or any other market that can be charted.

What separates this methodology from many other computer-generated trading systems is that this is *not* a 100 percent mechanical "black box" system. Rather, this book (and the multimedia associated with it) teach the individual how to apply the various trading signals to the style of trading with which he feels most comfortable. Position traders can trade the *trend* signals from the software, while short-term swing traders may prefer to take minor signals generated along the way—even trading *within* a trend, if desired. If you are uncertain which trading style might best suit you, the "ART Profile" exercise in this book will aid you in determining the style best suited to your personality.

Risk control is stressed throughout—determining effective position size, setting stop-loss exits, and more. Exact entry and exit points are given with the signals, so that you can judge your risk beforehand, and therefore determine position size as well. One of the many unique features is that stops are based on market conditions (chart patterns and volatility) as opposed to an arbitrary dollar amount. Therefore, the stops are more logical in terms of market mechanics, which prevents one from being stopped out prematurely, as might happen with "percentage risk" stops.

Finally, the techniques can be applied to option trading as well. I have long espoused the idea that any successful stock trading technique can be translated into a profitable option trading strategy, as long as one acts rationally in choosing the expiration month and striking price of the options to be purchased.

This multimedia approach to learning may be new to many readers, but the concepts and techniques associated with the ART software are well-suited to such an approach, and the benefits should be great for those who are willing to embrace the ART methodology and fit it into their "trading personality."

—LAWRENCE G. MCMILLAN
Author, *McMillan on Options*,
2nd Edition

Preface

This book, *The ART® of Trading*, is a unique opportunity for you, the trader or investor, to benefit from four fabulous things:

1. A sound trading system and software (Applied Reality Trading or ART) that gives you high probability entries, exits, and risk control—you get a free 30-day trial of the ART software with this book
2. Live streaming data direct from the markets to provide you with the truth and the reality of the financial markets—you get a free 30-day trial of live data with this book
3. The education on how to use the first fabulous two to generate profits
4. Superb brokerage services to execute your trades and investments once you have mastered the ART system

Best of all, you get this right here in just one book. This means that for the price of one book, you will be able to experience the reality of technical analysis software and data to generate greater profits. You'll see firsthand how technical analysis can enhance your fundamental analysis. Or, if you do not use fundamentals, you will see how ART can be used as a stand-alone decision maker for your trading and investing.

Maybe you are currently making entry and exit decisions by looking at fundamental information that you can gather from news, corporate earnings, Fed statistics, or any other multitude of reports that are available to you on CNBC and in the *Wall Street Journal*.

The reality is that those reports can be subject to distortion (a corporation carefully manages how the numbers are revealed so as to look their best); exaggeration (it's a slow news day and a commentator may need to enhance a story to make it newsworthy); and, of course, interpretation (a trader interprets a poor earnings report and panics out of a position to find out that the stock goes up, and up and up).

How do we determine what is reality? How do we know when something is exaggerated or distorted? How do we make sense of the information and the world around us to determine how to make profitable financial decisions? That is where "reality-based" trading and investing come in. ART, Applied Reality Trading, can help you decipher the information that you receive from the market so that you can clearly understand it and act on it intelligently.

This does not mean that you will be following someone else's reality. Instead, you will be creating your own reality and personal financial approach that works for you and makes you profits. Think about Columbus setting off to sail into the distance in 1492, when everyone else thought that the world was flat. That didn't stop Christopher; he had his own reality, and he followed it and succeeded. Despite the naysayers, he was courageous enough to try a new approach—which is what you will be doing. You will be an explorer and you will discover your reality, and you will use that as your edge in the financial markets.

The gift that ART and technical analysis can also give to you is clarity. You can include the ART trading software in your approach to confirm, or deny, an entry or exit. ART gives you the reality because it is based on the truths of the market—price and volume—and these cannot be distorted.

My personal approach happens to be purely technical analysis using the ART software, but many of my students do combine fundamentals with ART. You will decide what is right for you, and this book is designed to bring you up to speed in trading with ART® and technical analysis. If you have never used technical analysis and charts to make better entry and exit choices, there is no time like the present! This book, *The ART of Trading*, gives you everything you need to get started.

Enjoy the benefits of "reality-based" trading and technical analysis. I wish you all the best in everything that you do!

BENNETT MCDOWELL
San Diego, California
January 2008

Acknowledgments

T hank you to David Pugh at John Wiley & Sons for discovering us in New York City in February 2007. David, you are a master of the art of publishing, and without you this book would not be possible. Your gift of knowing how to bring the pages together to make them the best they could be is greatly appreciated. And, thanks to Stacey Small (David's right-hand assistant) for her patience, kindness, and many hours of expert templating. Also thank you to Larry McMillan, a friend and brilliant trader, for writing the Foreword.

TradeStation was one of the first two compatible platforms that the ART software was available on when released in 2003. A huge thank you to Janette Perez for her support of *The ART® of Trading* and for letting her TradeStation clients know about the value of using the TradeStation platform with the ART software and system. Also, thanks to Ray Fitzgerald at eSignal data services (also one of the first two platforms available for ART) for giving our clients that personal service they have come to appreciate over the years.

Also, I'd like to send a warmhearted thank you to Peter Smith at TD AmeriTrade. The newest ART platform available as of today is Quote-Tracker (which makes ART compatible with TD AmeriTrade), and, Peter, you made that into a reality. Your persistence and creativity are an inspiration. Another new platform is NinjaTrader, which has expanded our compatibility tremendously, and thanks to Raymond Deux for making that a smooth integration.

So many folks have helped us along the way, and I'd like to send a special thank you out to: Ed Schramm and Yves Pittleoud. Your friendship and support have made the journey a fun and rewarding one. And, of course, thanks to our many wonderful clients who have helped to shape the educational content we've developed since 1998.

Last, but most certainly not least, thanks to the women in my life. To my mother, Frances McDowell: Thank you for your encouragement, support, and love every step of the way—and also for being so nice. And to my wife, Jean McDowell, for your love, for taking care of the kids, and for being my best friend and a great partner all in one.

My deepest thanks go to all of you for making my journey a fun and exciting one!

Disclaimer

The information in *The ART® of Trading* is intended for educational purposes only. Traders and investors are strongly advised to do their own research and testing to determine the validity of any trading idea or system.

Trading in the financial markets involves substantial risk and TradersCoach.com, Bennett A. McDowell, or affiliates assume no responsibility for your success or failure in trading or investing in the markets. For this reason you should only use money you can afford to risk. Furthermore, past performance does not guarantee future results. Thus, even if you were successful with your trading and investing in the past, you may not be successful in the future. TradersCoach.com and Bennett A. McDowell make no performance representation or guarantee of any kind or nature. TradersCoach.com encourages you to conduct your own research and engage in numerous practice trades prior to risking any actual money.

Hypothetical or simulated performance results have certain inherent limitations. Unlike an actual performance record, simulated results do not represent actual trading. Also, since trades have not actually been executed, results may have under- or overcompensated for the impact, if any, of certain market factors, such as lack of liquidity. Simulated trading programs and ideas in general are also subject to the fact that they are designed with the benefit of hindsight. No representation is being made that any account will or is likely to achieve profits or losses similar to those discussed.

Introduction

O ne of the benefits of purchasing this book is that you will be able to experience firsthand the value of trading with the Applied Reality Trading software free by using your 30-day trial that is included with the book. This is a unique opportunity for you to get in the driver's seat and test drive the software on the markets and time frames you like to trade.

Plus, the software is ideal for any market and any time frame, which means whether you are an investor, day trader, or position trader, Applied Reality Trading will give you exact entries and exits into the market and will take the guess work out of your finances. This introduction outlines briefly how the book is laid out and what the companion DVD video program will do to help you with your trading and investing.

APPLIED REALITY TRADING IS KNOWN AS ART

The ART® of Trading will introduce you to a new way of trading and investing with a technical analysis system called Applied Reality Trading. Also known as ART, this system is a comprehensive trading methodology including software that labels the ART signals on financial charts so that you can easily see exact trade entries and exits. In addition, the software has voice technology that alerts you when to enter trades and exit trades.

The ART software is easy to use, and it processes complex algorithms and market information to give you high-probability trades and investment information. ART answers the questions of when to buy and when to sell. ART also answers the question of how to protect yourself from large losses by using effective risk control and money management.

While ART adds structure to your trading and investing, it also allows you the flexibility to tailor it to your personal style and experience level. You can use ART to trend trade, scalp, or countertrend trade. Or you can use the system to time your investments. ART is capable of doing all this since it is not a "black box" (100 percent mechanical) trading system.

The flexibility built into Applied Reality Trading allows you to integrate your financial beliefs with ART to create your own unique system that allows you to be a true artist in the financial markets. That is when you can become a master of the "Art of Trading."

REVOLUTIONARY LEARNING EXPERIENCE

You are about to embark on a revolutionary learning experience—one that will simplify the financial markets for you, and very well may simplify how you live your life. With Applied Reality Trading, you will learn how to focus on *reality*. The entire ART program is built around six major concepts:

1. No one can predict the markets with any true consistency.
2. To be a successful trader and investor you must look at the current market reality as it is happening and not rely on opinions, theories, or fantasies about what will happen.
3. The market will tell you exactly how to trade and invest, if you know how to listen to what it is saying.
4. Money management is essential.
5. Obtaining "the trader's mind-set" is a prerequisite for trading and investing with any approach or system to be successful.
6. Successful trading and investing requires that you align your unique personality with your chosen system.

The ART of Trading will show you how to use these six concepts to help improve your performance. Have an open mind as you process the material. Some concepts may challenge the inner core of your current belief system. While you read this book, try to be open-minded and receptive so you can fully explore the possibilities of Applied Reality Trading.

THE "ART PIE"

Trading and investing can be divided into four major areas. Think of an apple pie cut into four slices, and call this your "ART Pie." In order to be successful, you will need to understand and master each piece of pie. See Figure I.1.

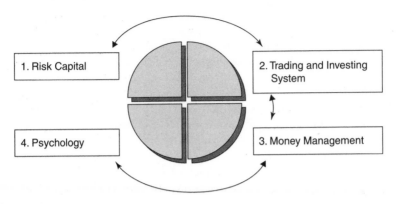

FIGURE I.1 ART Pie

This is where so many people fail. They do not master the entire pie. Look at the pie diagram. If you master your system but do not master money management, you will have a hard time winning. If you do not work with true "risk capital" (money you can afford to lose), then you are more susceptible to emotional trading and investing. You need to be proficient in every slice of the "ART Pie"!

This book will show you how to master all four slices of the "ART Pie."

LAYOUT OF THIS BOOK AND DVD VIDEO

The book is laid out into five parts plus the companion DVD so that you can quickly find the right information as you travel along the path of Applied Reality Trading. Here is a summary of the parts so you will have an understanding of where to look for what you need at any given point along your journey:

Part I: Reality

The ART system is based on reality, and here you will find specifics on how to use reality to improve your financial performance. With technical analysis and live streaming data from the markets, you will see how to minimize distortions in your financial decision making. By using price and volume, the true realities of the market, ART enables you to find consistent high-probability entries and exits that are not based on opinion. Plus, you will learn about the reality of financial risk and how to effectively manage that risk to generate greater profits.

Part II: Art

ART is an acronym for Applied Reality Trading. It is a fitting acronym since the Applied Reality Trading philosophy is built on being able to use the science of technical analysis and combine it with the art of your unique financial approach. Each of us has a different belief system that affects the way that we look at the financial markets. Given the right tools to start with, you must use your own creativity to master the tools and make them work for you. Much of this has to do with your financial psychology and self-awareness.

Part III: Science and Math

Science and math play an important role in financial success. The science of technical analysis combined with the math of proper money management is crucial. By using these concepts and integrating them into your own creative approach you will be able to develop a superior personal system based on what works for you.

Part IV: ART System Basics

This section lays the groundwork for using the ART software. In a very straightforward style, you will learn everything you will need to use ART. For both the novice and the master alike, Part IV shows you how to use the software to determine entries, exits, and risk control. You'll see how to use the flexibility of the software to customize your approach to suit your specific financial needs.

Part V: Advanced Techniques

It is recommended that you master Part IV before delving into the advanced techniques in this section. These techniques are best used by more experienced traders and investors. With that said, these advanced techniques are a gold mine of ideas, any one of which can boost your bottom line dramatically. It is highly recommended that you paper-trade these techniques before going into the market live with real money.

Companion DVD Video Program

On the inside back cover of the book is a DVD video program that will bring the ART software to life. In this DVD video you will benefit from a variety of material including classroom training with the author that will clarify and bring home all the concepts outlined in the book.

ALL CHARTS IN THIS BOOK WERE CREATED WITH THE eSIGNAL ART PLATFORM

Unless otherwise noted, all ART charts shown throughout this book were created using the eSignal ART platform. These charts are used here with the permission of eSignal.

You will note various icons such as triangles, squares, and diamond shapes on these charts. Generally, all of the ART platforms create a very similar appearance and function in the same way.

Note to TradeStation users: Your charts will have circles to identify the ART reversal bars instead of squares and diamonds. The ART software user's manual that you download upon registering for your free ART software trial will have complete information so that you will be able to easily read your charts with this minor variation in the visual icons.

A NOTE ABOUT DATA FEEDS AND YOUR 30-DAY FREE TRIAL OF THE ART SOFTWARE

Each of you reading this book may select a different ART platform, which may provide you with a different data feed to use with your free 30-day trial of the ART software. It is important for you to understand that due to very slight variations on data supply from each of the data suppliers available to you, if you ran two different platforms side by side on the same market and same time frame, you might possibly on occasion have different ART signals appear on your chart.

The software, if it receives different input, may produce different signals. This is not due to any change or modification of the ART software; it is only due to each live data provider's input, which may vary slightly from provider to provider.

FIGURES ARE INCLUDED ON THE DVD IN COLOR

The charts in this book are best read in full color. We have reproduced them in the text to allow you to follow the concepts as they are described—without interruption. To enhance the reader experience, we have also included all of these charts on the accompanying DVD. Though the material can certainly be understood without color, we have placed an icon next to text where we believe the reader will most benefit from referring to the DVD.

Also, please note that we have provided the ART® Chart Number for each of the figures. This reference will be of use for all TradersCoach.com subscribers.

Hopefully, this introduction has given you a brief understanding of *The ART of Trading*. I'd like to personally welcome you to the world of reality-based trading. If you have any questions or comments as you journey along *The ART of Trading*, feel free to call us at 858-695-0592 or e-mail me via Team@TradersCoach.com.

After a certain high level of technical skill is achieved, science and art tend to coalesce in esthetics, plasticity, and form. The greatest scientists are always artists as well...

—*Albert Einstein*

PART I

Reality

CHAPTER 1

It's All About Reality

REALITY-BASED TRADING AND INVESTING

Applied Reality Trading—ART—is all about reality. The foundation of this technical analysis system and software is built on the realities of the market—price and volume—and the entire philosophy is centered on facing the honest truth about your money and the markets.

Now, reality can be an elusive thing. Our perceptions can sometimes get in the way and cloud what deep down we know to be true. This is why it is important to constantly focus on looking to the heart of the matter to find the truth and the reality of every situation, market, and methodology that we encounter.

We may sometimes be seduced by illusions. As humans, it is hard to resist a charming and convincing offer of "... an easy profession that takes little to no investment of capital but rewards you with big profits instantly...." You've seen the infomercials on television. Sounds good enough, don't you think? But in your heart you know that if it sounds too good to be true, it probably is too good to be true. And it can be a tough pill to swallow when you realize that the fantasy you invested in may be unobtainable.

How about if we take a different approach? Instead of chasing fantasies (that with common sense we know are not true), how about if we follow our dreams and make them come true, and make them into reality? The distinction is that a dream is a genuine goal with realistic opportunity. It might require work and perseverance, but it is well worth the investment once you create the reality toward which you are working.

That is what this book is all about.

We want you to realize your financial goals and dreams and make them into realities by using concrete tools based on the realities of the market. You will learn about money management and risk control so that every step of the way you are on solid ground with an intelligent plan—designed by you specifically for your personal needs.

TAKE ART FOR A TEST DRIVE!

This book offers you a unique opportunity to test-drive the ART technical analysis software for 30 days. This way, you can see how trading the realities of the market with sound risk control and state-of-the-art software can significantly enhance your trading and investing profitability.

Whether you have experience with technical analysis or not, you'll have a chance to apply these ART techniques to your own trading and financial plan. You'll see the benefits of obtaining high-probability entry and exit signals that the ART software will provide you in your trading and in your investing.

Our Applied Reality Trading clients are a diverse group, including many very sophisticated hedge fund managers around the world that use the ART software to manage multimillions of dollars. Then, at the other end of the spectrum, we have many individual investors who just want more control over their own finances by getting reliable signals based on reality. And the beauty of the software is that it works on any time frame and in any market. This flexibility enables you to change markets when you want to and to use it for both day trading and investing.

What we will do in the following chapters is take you step by step through the ART methodology and system so that you will have all the tools and knowledge you need to benefit from a reality-based financial approach and software tool.

YOUR THOUGHTS CREATE YOUR REALITY

You will not develop the trader's mind-set, which is the "Holy Grail" to trading and investing until you master your mind!

THE IMPORTANCE OF THOUGHTS

Our thoughts shape our beliefs, which create our reality. In trading, this has profound implications. If we think or have a nagging thought that we may fail, then we create the seed that shapes our beliefs and manifests failure, all because we just think it!

High achievers maintain a philosophy that failure is not an option and that it pays to be a winner! They think of positive outcomes and "see" themselves as being successful.

Traders and investors who experience thoughts of failure should not take them lightly. Instead, they must find out what is causing these thoughts and take action to nullify them. Traders who fear failure will ultimately fail. Traders who fear success will not succeed. If you have these thoughts, then don't trade until these thoughts are dealt with and you are able to control them. You must confront them and remove their power so they don't occupy your thoughts.

Fear of failing, or fear of success, must be dealt with and removed from your thoughts before you will be successful at anything you try and do. If fear remains in thought and is energized by emotions that cause stress and anxiety, it will have an impact on your beliefs and ultimately manifest itself as your reality. It will sabotage you until your worst fear is realized—failure!

IT ALL STARTS WITH A THOUGHT!

Your thoughts shape your beliefs!

And your beliefs in turn shape your thoughts!

Your beliefs shape your emotions such as fear and greed!

Emotions such as fear and greed are relative, based on your unique beliefs!

Fear and greed drive markets and life itself!

Ultimately, you live your beliefs, which create your reality!

Trading is nothing more than a vehicle you choose to create your reality by trading your beliefs!

So choose and protect your thoughts carefully!

LIVE MARKET DATA

When trading with the ART software, you will be using minute-by-minute live streaming data that will be delivered to you from the market on which you decide to work. There is no greater reality in the universe than your live market data.

It will tell you the current price and volume any minute, any day, and any year. There is no middle man (other than your data provider) that will distort the data, no news announcer on television to "interpret" the data for you by adding their own opinions to the formula. Nope, your live streaming market data is the real thing. You'll be able to lay your eyes on the unaltered truth.

CHAPTER 2

The Reality of Price and Volume

There is no greater reality in trading than price and volume. These are facts, not opinions, and they cannot be distorted or misrepresented. They are what they are and what you see is what you get, as Flip Wilson used to say. WYSIWYG—isn't that an acronym in computer land these days? Anyway, what you will begin to see as you study the ART system and reality-based trading is that price and volume are your most valuable tools in reading the market.

WHY ARE PRICE AND VOLUME REALITY?

Price and volume are the reality of the market; everything else is a man-made measuring device that will most likely form destructive opinions. Some people believe that measuring devices form a road map. However, do we have a road map of our life in advance of our life? I don't think so. We may have a plan or fantasy about where we want to go, but until it happens, it is still just a fantasy.

THE CASE FOR SIMPLICITY IN A TRADING SYSTEM

The number of trading indicators, oscillators, and information sources available today is astounding. The reality is that "less is more." If you allow yourself to be inundated with unnecessary information and clutter, you will be drawn further away from the "truths" of the market—price and volume.

Simplicity will be the secret to your success. The ART system will simplify your trading and add structure, which helps to lessen anxiety that can lead to emotional trading.

The ART software is sophisticated, taking into account complex market dynamics and performing highly intricate calculations to deliver high-probability trades. Its genius lies in the way it illustrates this information with clear trade entries and exits.

Let me tell you a little about my trading and how I came to develop the ART system. My story may even resemble some of your trading experiences.

When I started, I read every book and examined virtually every trading system imaginable. From oscillators to powerful neural network computers, I studied it all. The one thing I found was that most systems tried to predict the market—and most failed miserably!

It seems the more we try to predict the market, the more it can't be done. Just as we cannot predict future life and world events, we cannot predict future market events. The fantasy that many traders believe in is that we can predict the future of price activity. The reality is that we cannot. Hopefully, I'm not bursting any bubbles out there, but better to hear it now than lose a ton of money later!

The most successful traders fully understand this concept, accept it, believe it, and implement it. They trade based on the current reality in the market versus the fantasy. Master traders grasp the concept of risk and probabilities in trading. They recognize and respect the concept of money management and stop-loss setting. In addition, they understand that trading is both a science and an art.

If trading were just science, you could buy a mechanical trading system, start it, walk away, and come back and be rich. If a "black box" system did exist, it would be so expensive that you and I could not afford to buy it. In fact, it would probably be kept so secret that we would not know it existed! Don't get me wrong—there are some good technical science "tools" on the market today, but remember, they are tools only, not the "Holy Grail."

DANGEROUS OPINIONS AND INDICATORS: A WORD ABOUT MACD AND STOCHASTICS

When I began trading, my indicators indeed gave me signals that prices or trends may change, but they did very little to help me consistently time those changes accurately enough to make money. Instead, these indicators caused me to form counterproductive opinions.

Three examples that show how opinions and indicators can be dangerous:

1. Opinion—MACD Example:

    Let's say you have bullish divergence in a moving average convergence/divergence (MACD) oscillator, and you now have an opinion in your mind that prices should change from the current downtrend to an uptrend.

    So, you look for a reason to go long, an entry signal. One comes along and you take it. You think to yourself that you would not have normally taken that signal if you did not see bullish divergence, but with bullish divergence you feel you should. Prices then continue downward even lower and the bullish divergence remains bullish so you stay with your long position.

    "... Can't go much lower ..." you say to yourself. It does go lower and now you're worried but you do not want to sell and take the large loss, so you hold on. After all, the MACD divergence is still bullish, but not as much as before.

    Soon the divergence turns into no divergence and instead the trend down becomes apparent, and you now must sell out. You feel depressed, frustrated, and betrayed by your MACD oscillator! If the oscillator had not been there, you would never have taken the trade to begin with.

2. Opinion—Stochastic Example:

    You get a trading signal to go long, but this time your stochastic oscillator indicates that prices are overbought already, so you do not take the long position. The so-called overbought stochastic oscillator formed an opinion in your mind not to take the trade. Now you sit there and watch a great uptrend developing right before your eyes and the stochastic oscillator remains overbought during the entire 10-point uptrend. Had you never looked at the stochastic oscillator, you would not have had an opinion, and would have gone long.

3. Opinion—MACD Example:

    You see bearish divergence on the MACD oscillator, so you form an opinion that the uptrend is ending and now you look to get out of your long position right away. You then use a trailing stop and exit the market—only to find prices reverse and go higher and the MACD oscillator turn bullish. You are left scratching your head.

Examples of how opinions distort reality could go on and on, but you get the idea. And the idea is that oscillators form opinions, and opinions are not in the best interest of the successful trader. Instead, with ART, you will learn to listen to what the market is actually saying through price action and volume.

Strive to create an environment without opinions. That means avoid reading financial newspapers, watching financial TV, or listening to financial news in any form while trading.

News programs form opinions, trading oscillators form opinions, and market analysts form opinions. We do not know how the markets will react to news and financial recommendations. If we think we do, then we are forming an opinion about the news.

How many times have companies come out with great earnings and sold off right after the announcement. And when the market does sell off, the news commentator comes out and says "... the stock had run up already in expectation of the good numbers and then sold off...." If instead the stock continued upward, the news commentator would say, "... good earnings drove the market upward...." News commentators operate on 20/20 hindsight. We do not have this luxury.

OVERBOUGHT AND OVERSOLD CONDITIONS

The Market Itself Is Never Overbought or Oversold—Think about It

Markets work to bring price in line with supply and demand. Markets are perfectly efficient. If supply always equals demand, then how can a market be overbought or oversold? It may be expensive, but *expensive* can be a relative term.

For example, suppose you purchased a painting by a currently unknown artist/painter for $1,000. The next week your artist/painter gets reviewed in a famous magazine and his work is now nationally recognized, so your painting increases in value to $1,500. Some say that your painting is too expensive or that prices are now overbought because it went up in value too quickly in just one week.

What if the next week a famous collector buys a similar painting by the same artist/painter for $4,000, and now the value of your painting increases to $3,000!

All the indicators said that it was overbought at $1,500 because the price went up too high in a short period of time. The reality is that because of supply and demand, prices are exactly where they should be—regardless of the reasons! There is no such thing in an efficient market as overbought and oversold. Prices are where they are because that is where they are supposed to be!

INEFFICIENT MARKETS VERSUS EFFICIENT MARKETS

There's a great debate between academics regarding the issue of efficient markets versus inefficient markets. There are traders who believe that just because they make money in the markets, the markets are therefore inefficient. Their belief is that they exploit the inefficiencies of the market in order to make money.

But, aren't they just adding to the efficiency and liquidity of the market with each and every trade they make? For every one of those traders who made money in the market, there is another trader on the other side of the trade who lost money. Now, that is efficient. The bottom line is the markets are efficient no matter how you look at it.

SUPPLY = DEMAND

When supply equals demand, both the seller and the buyer disagree on value, but agree on price. This is important...

When this happens, it is a truth in the marketplace. The amount of supply and demand occurring in the market is called *volume*. That also is a truth. Both price and volume are absolute and are truths of the market because they are not distorted. (Indicators used in technical analysis often distort price and volume.)

CHAPTER 3

Managing Risk: Always Set a Stop-Loss Exit

Setting stop-loss exits is the first step in managing your risk. There are a multitude of other techniques, but the first line of defense for you will be to learn how to set effective stops and then to learn how to adhere to those stops.

THE NEED FOR MONEY MANAGEMENT

Please understand the risks in trading the financial markets and live in full awareness. Let your positive beliefs lead you to take the actions necessary to succeed.

For traders to blindly enter the markets and trade simply because they are thinking positive thoughts is to ignore the full spectrum of what is possible. However, to live in constant fear of losing will cause you to trade the financial markets with fear, anxiety, negativity, and aggression, which are equally destructive.

Instead, acknowledge both sides of the coin, the good and the bad. React to market activity with full awareness and pay close attention to your risk control. Then you will create a positive reality with a feeling of abundance and goodwill. By acknowledging the good and the bad—the reality—and by fine-tuning your money management system, you are on your way to greater prosperity.

A TRADER'S MONEY MANAGEMENT SYSTEM

Money management is a rather in-depth topic and I recommend that you use *A Trader's Money Management System: How To Ensure Profit And Avoid The risk Of Ruin* (John Wiley & Sons, 2008), a book I wrote to cover this topic in depth. It will enable you to manage your risk in every way from learning how to refine your stops, to record keeping and analysis with The Trader's Assistant™, to understanding the risk-of-ruin tables and how to determine what is the right amount of capital to risk on each and every trade. You will probably get the best price on Amazon.com and I urge you to continue in your quest for money management tools since that is where you will be able to further increase your profits.

ACCEPTING RISK

Before you can effectively accept risk in your finances, you must first completely believe that there is a true benefit to you in doing so. This inner belief very often comes after having experienced the power of the markets in the form of a painful and substantial monetary loss. Regardless of how you ultimately develop the motivation to manage your risk, it is imperative that you do so.

There are six primary types of risk you need to accept:

1. *Trade risk* is the "calculated" risk you take on each trade. With ART, your risk will never be more than 2 percent on any given trade. You will maintain this 2 percent risk by adjusting your trade size and setting a stop-loss exit. Advanced traders, see "Important Note" on page 78.

2. *Market risk* is the inherent risk of being in the market. This type of risk involves the entire gamut of risk possible when in the markets. Market risk can exceed trade risk. For this reason, ART traders never actively trade more than 10 percent of their net worth. Market risk encompasses catastrophic world events and crashes that paralyze markets. Events causing market "gaps" in price against your trade position is an example of market risk.

3. *Margin risk* involves risk where you can lose more than the dollar amount in your margined trading account. You would then *owe* your brokerage firm money if your trade goes against you.

4. *Liquidity Risk*. If there are no buyers when you want to sell, you will experience the inconvenience of liquidity risk. In addition to the inconvenience, this type of risk can be costly when the price is going straight

down to zero and you are not able to get out, much like the experience of Enron shareholders in the year 2001.

5. *Overnight Risk* for day traders, presents a concern in that what can happen overnight when the markets are closed, and can dramatically impact the value of their position. There is the potential to have a "Gap Open" at the opening bell, when the price is miles away from where it closed the day before.

6. *Volatility Risk* can present a bumpy market that may tend to stop you out of trades repeatedly creating significant draw down. This occurs when your stop-loss exits are not in alignment with the market and are not able to breathe with current price fluctuations.

Risk is inevitable in the markets and there is an art to managing the possibilities. It is not a matter of fearing the risk; instead, focus on playing the "what if" scenario so that you can adequately prepare yourself for any outcome.

SEVEN BASIC STOPS

A stop-loss exit, or a stop, is a predetermined exit point you will select prior to entering the market. Designing an effective stop-loss approach will be crucial to increasing your profit potential.

If your trade or investment goes against you, a stop-loss approach enables you to cut your losses quickly so that you have capital with which to reenter the market. The alternative to using an effective stop-loss strategy is to sustain severe and devastating losses at one point or another. The market is unforgiving in this regard, and ignoring the inevitable is to tempt fate and invite painful financial loss into your portfolio or trading account.

Following are seven of the most common stop approaches:

1. *Initial stop.* This stop is set at the beginning of your trade and entered as you enter the market. The initial stop is also used to calculate your position size. It is the largest loss you will take in the current trade.

2. *Trailing stop.* This stop develops as the market develops. This stop enables you to lock in profit as the market moves in your favor.

3. *Resistance stop.* This stop is a form of trailing stop used in trends. It is placed just under countertrend pullbacks in a trend

4. *Three-bar trailing stop.* This stop is used in a trend if the market seems to be losing momentum and you anticipate a reversal in trend.

5. *One-bar trailing stop.* This stop is used when prices have reached your profit target zone or when you have a breakaway market and want to lock in profits, usually after three to five price bars moving strongly in your favor.

6. *Trend line stop.* A trend line is placed under the lows in an uptrend or on top of the high in a downtrend. You want to get out when prices close on the other side of the trend line.

7. *Regression channel stop.* Very similar to a regular trend line, the regression channel forms a nice channel between the highs and lows of the trend and usually represents the width of the trend channel. Stops are placed outside the low of the channel on uptrends and outside the high of the channel in downtrends. Prices should close outside the channel for the stop to be taken.

Other stops used are generally a form of one of the above stops or a derivative of them. Setting stops will require judgment by you, the trader. Judgment is based on experience and the type of trader you are. You will set your stops based on your psychology and comfort level. If you find you are getting stopped out too frequently or if you seem to be getting out of trends too early, then chances are you are trading from a fearful mindset. Try and let go of your fear and place stops at reasonable places in the market.

Position your stops in relation to market price activity, and don't pick an arbitrary place to set your stop. Many traders incorrectly buy and sell the same number of shares each time they trade. Then they choose a stop so their loss is the same dollar amount each time they are stopped out. By doing this, they are disregarding the meaningful market support and resistance areas where stops should be set.

Remember, the ART software does an excellent job of identifying stop signals, which are identified by choosing key levels of support and resistance. This enables you to set stops that are in alignment with current market dynamics.

NOT SETTING STOPS

If you do not use stops, you are setting yourself up for failure. When trading stocks, for example, if you do not use stops and hang on to losing trades to a point where you emotionally feel you cannot exit the trade because the loss is so large, you are doomed.

If this happens, you are "married" to that stock and it may not be a stock you really want to own as an investment. Some stocks we trade are good for short-term trades only because we are taking advantage of the momentum in the stock. It may be a stock we would never invest in and hold for a long time.

If you find yourself wishing for a stock to turn around, you're not trading well. Based on the reasons you entered the trade and the location of your stop, you should always know in a second whether you should be in or out of a trade.

WHAT HAPPENS WHEN YOU DON'T HAVE A STOP-LOSS EXIT STRATEGY?

Never trade without knowing exactly where you will get out if the trade goes against you. All large losses start as small, manageable losses. Let me share with you an e-mail I received from a trader visiting the Traders Coach.com web site. It illustrates the importance of using stops:

> *Dear Bennett,*
> *I received your e-mail and I think your techniques along with your software are fantastic. Unfortunately for me I am stuck in a bad trade where I was caught without a stop/loss in the March "BP" several weeks ago. I have lost so badly that I think I may have to fold up my trading tent and seek a job! I have been waiting for a reversal but I do not think one will materialize by expiration. I see a potential triple top forming but I do not know how long the funds will press the upside. I am looking for scalp trades in other markets with the little margin I have left so as to try and recoup something by expiration. If I am fortunate enough to survive, I will try to not make the same mistake again.*

I often receive calls from traders who either did not set a stop-loss or failed to get out of their trade when their stop was hit. They tell me that now they cannot get out because their loss would be too large to bear. If this is happening to you, then you do not yet have the trader's mind-set. You have to realize that being stopped out is a natural part of trading. You must accept this and not let it get you angry or upset.

Remember, it is better to cut your losses short. It is the only way you will be in a position to let your winners ride.

SETTING MENTAL STOPS

For some markets it is better not to put the stop actually in the market when you have the position on. Some market makers will see your stop, and if there are enough other traders with similar stops, the market makers may try and hit your stop. Then they make money and you do not. In markets like this, you can set a mental stop and get out immediately if it is hit. Be sure you have the psychological toughness to get out when you are supposed to. If you don't, then go ahead and enter the stop when you take the trade.

MOVING STOPS

Never move your stop for emotional reasons, especially when it is your initial stop. As new trailing stops are determined to lock in profit, you can move your stops based on newly confirmed Pyramid Trading Points and/or ART Reversals. If you add on to your winning trade (increase your trade size), your stop must be adjusted to control your risk in relation to your new trade size.

When adjusting your stop due to an increase in trade size, always adjust the stop closer to your current position to lower the risk in relation to your larger trade size. Once you do this, you should never roll back your stop, since now your larger trade size will warrant the tighter stop to maintain proper risk control.

Many students ask about moving stops based on different time frames. This is an advanced technique. As a general rule, always set your stops on the same time frame as you entered the trade. In other words, if you use a daily chart to base your trade entry, use the daily chart to set your initial stop.

There are exceptions to this, but only after you have developed enough experience. Become profitable using the same time frame first, then perhaps venture into multiple time frames later.

With the ART system, stops are set based on the realities of the market and should only be moved when the ART software designates new stop-loss exits.

CHAPTER 4

If It Sounds Too Good to Be True . . .

SYSTEM RATES OF RETURN ARE MEANINGLESS

There are many trading and investing systems on the market today. Some companies will boast fabulous returns and provide examples. How disappointing it is for you to find that even when you buy that system, those fabulous returns are usually unobtainable.

Just about every system can work profitably over an isolated period of time. It is consistency that counts. That can be misleading, too. Why? Because every trader and investor will implement the same system differently based on their own unique personality and belief system. Each individual will produce different returns on the same system. For these reasons, we do not state rates of return or performance results for the ART system.

Instead, ART will focus on solid money management, trading psychology, and a system that makes sense. We want you to concentrate on developing your skills so you can see how your own performance has the unlimited potential to improve. We'll give you the "tools" of the trade. The rest is up to you!

While ART will teach you how to trade and invest using the realities of the market, another aspect of the Applied Reality Trading program lies in its flexibility. You can tailor ART in accordance with your beliefs and personality. This means you can design your own ART approach. This can be a powerful force.

ART IS NOT A "BLACK BOX" SYSTEM

The reality is there is no such thing as a black box system. Some may tell you that their system can offer you a 100 percent mechanical solution that requires absolutely *no* discretionary decisions. The truth and reality is that these black box systems don't work well over time because they can't adapt to ever-changing market cycles. What you want to do is become a "master trader and investor," blending your beliefs with tools such as ART to produce a unique financial system that you can implement in any market conditions.

Master traders and investors use software as a tool (not a black box) to help them make financial decisions. Trading and investing is not that simplistic—there are far too many market variables for software alone to make all your decisions for you.

Master traders and investors have learned the necessary trading skills that encompass risk control, trading psychology, managing their response to fear and greed, discipline, and identifying the different types of market cycles and knowing how to adapt to them.

By the time you complete The ART of Trading program, you will have firsthand experience in how to integrate your belief system into your discretionary decisions to adapt to a variety of market conditions.

Markets move in cycles, and each time frame (even in the same market) can experience a different cycle as well. The primary cycles are Trending, Consolidating, Breaking Out of a Consolidation, and Corrective. Different cycles warrant different trading styles. This is why ART is not a black box system—you need to make adjustments to your ART style and adapt as the market changes. You need to adapt to changing market cycles.

The key to being consistently profitable is to master your trading skills in different market cycles. Markets can also experience volatility changes. Certain market cycles are accompanied by changes in volatility. A change in volatility can also be caused by traders on other time frames dominating that market. This can cause unexplained volatility on the time frame you are trading and may cause you to experience losses. You will need to learn how to use the ART software in a variety of market cycles and in relation to your own style.

WHY DO 90 PERCENT OF ALL TRADERS LOSE MONEY?

Trading the financial markets is rewarding, but it is also hard work. Developing your skills to a level where you are profitable on a consistent basis will take time and a lot of practice. During your practice stage, you will need to paper-trade to hone and develop your skills in a risk-free environment. Once you are profitable paper-trading, you will be ready to trade with real money. Most traders are unwilling to do this kind of work, which is why so many fail.

Don't let this 90 percent statistic intimidate you because the reality is that in most professions, only about 10 percent of the people make it to the top anyway. It is actually quite normal. Take, for example, the person who wants to play the piano. The first step is to buy a piano, take lessons, and practice. Many who start may not realize the commitment it will take to play well. In fact, when they find out how much time and practice and the number of lessons they will need, most give up. Also, some may not have a musical ear, or the ability or aptitude to master the piano. This is a good analogy for learning to trade because the commitment, ability, and aptitude to master trading is similar to that of learning to play the piano.

Playing music is the ability to integrating yourself with your musical instrument to create your own unique experience of expression. Trading is no different. The master trader or investor integrates his beliefs with his system or approach to create desired results.

CHAPTER 5

Personal Methods to Increase Trading Success

WRITE IN YOUR "SUNRISE TRADING JOURNAL"

The "Sunrise Trading Journal" is a "long" journal approach where you will write three long pages every morning at sunrise or when you first wake, prior to your trading day.

Begin writing in your journal every day from this day forward, including weekends. The purpose of this is so that you can start to develop an understanding of your feelings and your psychology. You will also see how this can improve your investing and trading performance. In addition, the routine of the journal creates instant structure and discipline in your trading and finances.

Before you begin your day, when you first wake up, go to your Sunrise Trading Journal and write down your feelings, thoughts, and ideas. They don't have to be trading or investing related and can basically ramble on as a stream of consciousness. The idea is to empty your mind of any distractions and do a "mind dump."

This will enable you to focus on the reality of the present moment and to work in the here and now. If you have no thoughts or emotions, just write down that you "have no thoughts or emotions."

The goal is to capture whatever unconscious information you can gather when you first wake up and then release it onto the handwritten page. Then you've transferred any distracting unconscious baggage into your journal before you start your work day. You will find it enlightening, and it will clear your mind.

After writing for one full month, review your journal and use a colored highlighter marker to highlight any recurring words or themes you find. Look for patterns in your writing and in your thoughts, as well as any changes from the time you first began writing in your journal. Do you see any themes of anger, fear, or greed? Are your journal entries changing from negative themes to more positive ones? Reviewing in this way will lead you to discover clues about yourself and ways to improve your trading and investing.

Repeat this process every month.

ENTER A "CONTRACT FOR SUCCESS"

Complete your "Contract for Success" today (see pages 25 and 26). It is important for you to make the inner commitment to be successful.

By entering into this written contract, you are physically and emotionally encouraging yourself to attain trading and financial success. At the same time, you are promising yourself that you will use planning and risk control in your trading and investing; you will set stops and adhere to these stops, and you will do the work necessary to become successful.

Ultimately, you are telling yourself you will have the perseverance to be a winner. If you don't truly believe you can be a winner, you won't be.

FAX OR MAIL-IN "CONTRACT FOR SUCCESS"

TRADERSCOACH.COM   FAX: (858) 695-1397   PHONE: (858) 695-0592
ADDRESS: 10755-F Scripps Poway Parkway, #477, San Diego, CA 92131 USA

Student First Name:_____ Last Name:_____

Street Address: _____ P.O. Box: _____

City: _____ State:_____

Zip:_____ Country:_____

Phone:_____ Fax: _____

E-Mail:_____   @ _____

"Student" named above agrees to the following:

1.) Stop-Loss exits will be determined and calculated <u>PRIOR</u> to placing all financial trades and transactions.

2.) Stop-Loss exits will be adhered to on <u>EVERY</u> transaction executed. Get out of the transaction when your stop tells you to!

3.) Trading and investing in the financial markets pose a high financial risk and the student named in this contract will take full responsibility for any and all monetary risk they take upon themselves.

4.) The student named in this contract will only trade or invest with money they can afford to lose and will paper-trade until they have developed a profitable approach.

5.) Further, the student named in this contract will stop live trading with real money if they have a losing set of "25 Trades" (or a loss to their account in excess of 15%) and will evaluate the cause of the loss prior to re-entering the live market.

6.) In addition to the above five items the "Student" named above will follow the "Trading & Investing Rules" he or she has outlined on the back of this page.

Sign below to indicate your agreement with the above:

Student Signature: _____ Date: _____

Trading & Investing Buddy Signature: _____ Date: _____

GUIDELINES FOR COMPLETING YOUR "CONTRACT FOR SUCCESS"

1.) Through testing and "Paper Trading" determine what works best for you and outline your "Trading & Investing Rules" one by one; always focus on profitability.

2.) What time of day and what days of the week are best for your performance?

3.) Are there any physical requirements necessary for your success— such as enough sleep, eating right, discipline, etc?

4.) What privacy requirements do you need to eliminate and reduce distractions—such as no phone calls, no television, no visits from family and friends, etc?

5.) Specify your personal money management formula (over and above the need for stop-loss exits).

6.) Specify your technical specifics—such as what style of trading and investing you will be doing, what market time frame(s) you will be using, which financial market (s) you want to work on, etc.

7.) Write down any personal "Trading & Investing Rules" that you may have difficulty in adhering to (especially the ones that you know will make you more profitable).

8.) Update your contract once a year, or whenever you adapt your rules and you find it improves profitability.

9.) Find a "Trading & Investing Buddy," someone that can also sign-off on your contract and keep you "Honest." This would be someone you talk to often, not necessarily a trader or financial expert, but someone that knows you and can help keep you "On-Track"—such as your wife or husband, friend, someone you've met at a trading seminar, a "Trading Coach," etc. By keeping your buddy in the loop, it will enable you to maintain accountability for your actions and your results.

10.) After completing your "Contract For Success" be sure to FAX or MAIL it to the TradersCoach.com office. This will help your trading psychology since you will have made a written commitment to your "Trading & Investing Rules" and you will have a support team to help you implement these rules successfully.

CHAPTER 6

Identify Your Personal ART Profile

I t is important to examine your personality, in order to help you align the ART signals with your beliefs. One of the key strengths of the ART program is that you can align your beliefs with the ART signals and create your own approach. This will enable you to become a powerful force in the market.

Keep in mind that you will be determining your "current" ART profile as it exists in reality today. This profile may change over time as your beliefs and experience level change. Be sure to revisit this chapter from time to time to reevaluate your current reality.

EXPERIENCE LEVEL

Select one experience level that describes your *current* level of experience:

1. Master Level

The master has years of experience in the markets and is at an expert level of knowledge and skills. He understands his own beliefs and knows what strengths and weaknesses he has. He trades in accordance with his beliefs, personality, and temperament. He has an intuitive feel of the markets and operates in a controlled, calm, but fluid way, and in the "zone."

He understands and accepts risk and always operates with risk in mind, but is never paralyzed by it. He is not controlled by emotions such as fear and greed. He trades in total awareness and may at times seem to have a carefree attitude. He consistently weighs the risk-to-reward equation.

He can adjust his systems to be more profitable in different market cycles and can quickly determine which time frames and markets are best to maintain profitability. In other words, he can go from one winning cycle to another with minimal drawdown between winning cycles and can move at lightning speed if needed.

The master listens to and understands what the market is saying. He thinks of the market as a friend and enjoys the challenge and the process.

He is consistently profitable and represents the top 5 percent of all traders worldwide. Individuals at this level have the skill and experience to earn significant net revenue on a consistent basis. This is the level that most "get rich quick" advertisements claim you can achieve instantly with little or no capital.

Profit zone: The master is consistently generating 10 percent profit on his account every month over a period of at least 12 months.

2. Intermediate Level

The intermediate trader or investor is moderately profitable on a consistent basis, but emotions still get the best of him. He has developed enough skill to know what to do to be consistently profitable. He is not nearly as profitable as the master, but consistent enough to acknowledge that success is possible and realizes how important psychology is.

Personal development is still needed. This is what keeps the intermediate trader or investor from being a master. The whole body is not yet integrated with the market and the process. He occasionally has days where he feels and performs like a master, but not consistently.

He has varying forms of anxiety that cause problems. Besides not being as profitable, the difference between intermediate and the master is abstract. The difference is intangible or nonlinear; it has to do with the "art" of trading. The trader's mind-set is not as developed as the master.

Profit zone: The intermediate trader or investor is generally breaking even consistently or generating a small profit consistently.

3. Novice Level

This category encompasses everyone else who is not making money on a consistent basis for whatever reason—from beginners to those who "know it all" but still can't make consistent money in the markets. To get out of this category requires work on skills, market knowledge, emotional exploration, and practice.

It is important to paper-trade until you are consistently profitable. You need live experience during a variety of market conditions to experience drawdown and how it affects your psychology.

When paper-trading is consistently profitable, then and only then trade with real money. Novice traders and investors will remain stuck at this level if they take the "easy" route of rushing into the markets with real money before they are ready.

Diminishing the importance of paper-trading indicates impatience, compulsive behavior, gambling personality, a "get rich quick" mentality, and lack of discipline—all of which will keep you stuck at the novice level. You will be unprofitable on a consistent basis until you either acknowledge it is time to change or you give up and say that this is not for you.

Don't forget that every master started at this novice level! The length of time you spend here depends on how well you work on your emotional stability and development.

Profit zone: The novice is consistently losing dollars in his practice paper-trading (or in his live-trading in the market with actual dollars if he is currently live-trading).

TRADING STYLE

Select one style that describes your *current* method or style:

1. Trend Style

The trend trader or investor likes to trade with the overall trend regardless of time frame. He uses the Pyramid Trading Point for trend identification, trade entry, and trade exit and uses ART Reversals to "scale out" of trends or "scale in" to a trend trade. He rarely uses a stop and reverse (SAR).

Trends can be found on just about any time frame. Stops are adjusted or trailed just enough so the trader can stay with the trend even during corrections within the trend (can use trend lines and advanced techniques such as the Elliott Wave, and classic technical analysis).

A day trader could be classified in this category when trend-trading intraday time frames. Trend traders usually are not averse to authority figures, and they feel comfortable "belonging" versus being a "loner." These tendencies allow for a comfortable fit of going with the crowd of traders in a trend.

2. Scalp Style

Scalpers take quick profits using ART Reversals and minor Pyramid Trading Point trade entries. They use the SAR technique, and may either be long or short almost all the time while using SARs.

A scalper can be a day trader or position trader and can "scalp" with a trend or against a trend. Traders who are averse to authority figures tend to be better scalpers in the market. Scalpers like quick action, and need to be careful not to overtrade. They should also be careful with trading due to anxiety issues.

3. Countertrend Style

Countertrend traders trade the corrections of an established trend. These traders predominantly use ART Reversals to time their trades and exit the market. They can be day traders or position traders. The countertrend trader usually likes to be a "loner" and move independently and is averse to authority figures. He usually does not flow with the crowd and therefore tends to feel uncomfortable going with the crowd of traders in a trend.

TRADING FREQUENCY

(Select one trading frequency that describes your *current* time frame or frequency of trades):

1. Day Trader

The classic day trader opens and closes all his trades when the market is open during the trading period and does not hold positions overnight. Day traders usually use 1-minute to 5-minute charts. They can either use scalping techniques or be intraday trend traders.

There are three main reasons why day trading should be attempted by master traders rather than novice traders:

- When day trading, trading time is compressed. Losses and wins come at you faster and more often, which requires a mature, developed trading psychology.
- You must have the psychology to resist being seduced by the open market—you must remain emotionless and objective.
- Your day-trading results can be highly impacted by others trading on higher time frames; the lower your time frame, the greater the effect this will have on you.

2. Position Trader

These traders usually use daily charts, weekly charts, and 60-minute-interval charts to base their trading decisions on. Primarily trend traders, position traders hold positions until the trend is exhausted, and therefore they may hold a position for a few days, a few weeks, or even a few months if the trend can be maintained.

3. Investor

Investors are traders when they attempt to time their long-term investments. They study fundamentals and combine this with technical analysis. Investors are long-term trend traders using weekly, monthly, and yearly charts. They can deal with minor losses but are less comfortable with active trading, where losses can come quickly and frequently during drawdown.

ART PROFILES—HOW THEY WORK

ART profiles classify you so you can quickly identify what experience level, trading or investing style, and trading or investing frequency you fall into. This helps you determine what ART signals may be the best for you to use.

- Identify your experience level from the list in this chapter (master, intermediate, or novice).
- Identify your trading style from the list in this chapter (trend, scalp, or countertrend).
- Identify your trading frequency from the list in this chapter (day trader, position trader, or investor)

HOW TO VISUALIZE YOUR ART PROFILE

Draw a triangle; label it starting at the top and moving clockwise as:

- Experience
- Style
- Frequency

In the middle of the triangle, list the ART signals to use based on your experience level, trading style, and trading frequency. Use the sample profiles on the following pages to determine what ART signals will be best for you. When you have done this, you have matched your personality, beliefs, and skill level to the appropriate ART signals.

TABLE 6.1 ART Profiles

Profile	Experience	Style	Frequency
A	Novice	Trend	Position
B	Novice	Trend	Investor
C	Intermediate	Countertrend	Position
D	Intermediate	Scalping	Day trader
E	Master	Countertrend	Day trader
F	Master	Trend	Position

If you begin to trade and realize you misidentified yourself, make corrections to your ART profile. Then identify the ART signals based on your new ART profile.

Over time, your "ART profile will change as you develop and grow. As your profile changes, the ART signals you use may change to fit your new ART profile.

You will find sample profiles in this chapter as shown in Table 6.1.

The six sample profiles will fit many traders and investors, but are not all-inclusive, meaning you may create a unique profile outside these sample profiles. See Figure 6.1.

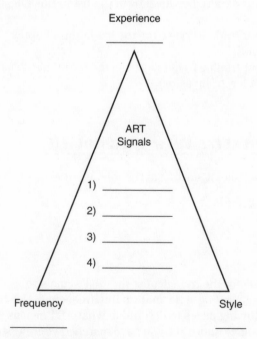

FIGURE 6.1 ART Profile Blank

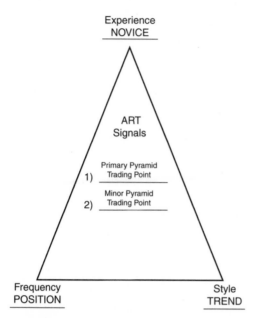

FIGURE 6.2 ART Profile "A"

ART Profile A indicates a novice/trend/position trader, as shown in Figure 6.2.

The ART signals you would use are the primary Pyramid Trading Point for primary trend determination for entries and exits, and the minor Pyramid Trading Point to identify corrections in the dominant trend only. As you gain experience, you will progress to Trading Profile F and begin to use additional ART signals.

Note: If you are a novice/trend/investor trader, your profile would be similar to Profile A because investors are also position traders but usually hold on to their positions for longer periods of time. Investors usually use longer-term charts for their analysis, such as the weekly and monthly charts.

ART Profile B indicates a novice/trend/investor, as shown in Figure 6.3.

The ART signal you would use is the primary Pyramid Trading Point to determine the primary trend, entries, and exits.

ART Profile C indicates an intermediate/countertrend/position trader, as shown in Figure 6.4.

The ART signals you would use are the primary Pyramid Trading Points to determine the primary trend entries and exits and ART One-Bar and Two-Bar Reversals for scaling in and scaling out of trends. Minor

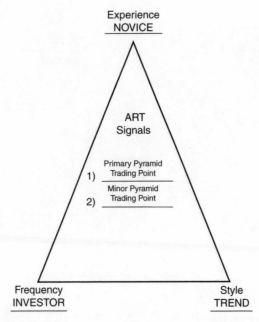

FIGURE 6.3 ART Profile "B"

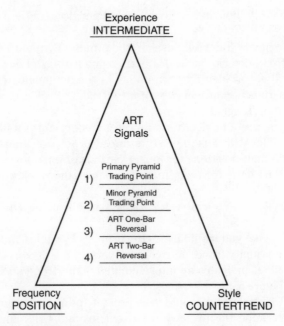

FIGURE 6.4 ART Profile "C"

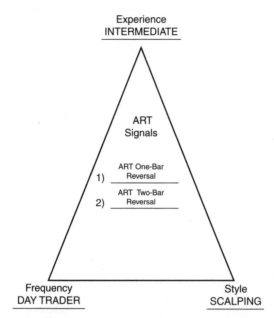

FIGURE 6.5 ART Profile "D"

Pyramid Trading Points could also be used to identify corrections in dominant trends, and in some cases catch a new trend in its early stages.

ART Profile D indicates an intermediate/scalping/day trader, as shown in Figure 6.5.

The ART signals you would use are the ART One-Bar and Two-Bar Reversals for scalping the markets between bullish and bearish ART Reversals.

Advanced variations of scalping would be to scalp in the direction of the primary trend as designated by a primary Pyramid Trading Point, or countertrend scalping is another option. (Your experience level when using these techniques would be master.)

ART Profile E indicates a master/countertrend/day trader, as shown in Figure 6.6.

The ART signals you would use are the primary Pyramid Trading Point to determine the primary trend, entries, and exits and the ART One-Bar and Two-Bar Reversals for countertrend trade entries and exits.

Minor Pyramid Trading Point formations could also be used for countertrend trading because they indicate correction in dominant trends, and in some cases can be used in conjunction with ART Reversals to catch countertrend trades.

ART Profile F indicates a master/trend/position trader, as shown in Figure 6.7.

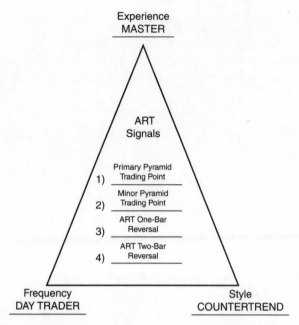

FIGURE 6.6 ART Profile "E"

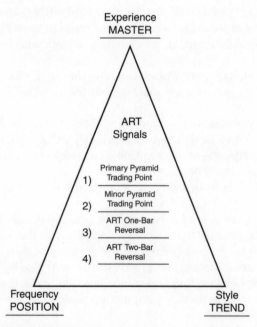

FIGURE 6.7 ART Profile "F"

The ART signals you would use are the primary Pyramid Trading Point to determine the primary trend with entries and exits and the ART One-Bar and Two-Bar Reversals for scaling in and scaling out of trends. The minor Pyramid Trading Point could also be used to identify corrections in dominant trends and in some cases catch a new trend in its early stages.

PART II

Art

CHAPTER 7

Design Your Business Plan

RUNNING YOUR TRADING AND INVESTING AS A REAL BUSINESS

Trading and investing is a real business—run it that way! Just like a restaurateur has accounting to do, food that spoils, overhead to pay, and needs sufficient capital, you will face similar business challenges. Food that spoils is like being stopped out of trades, money gone. Overhead to pay is like having to buy computers, Internet access, trading software, educational books like this one, quotes services, maybe an office, capital requirements, and so on.

Also, when you approach this as a business, your psychology will change to that of a professional—meaning that it is easier to be successful if you approach your trading and investing as a business rather than a hobby. To start, you may consider this venture a part-time business. You will feel better about yourself and will do the things you need to be doing to improve your performance.

YES, TRADERS AND INVESTORS ARE ARTISTS

Great musicians do not just start creating exceptional music. They learn about the science of music. They practice, practice, and practice more. They love what they do. They love the journey. It takes time, discipline, and persistence. Usually, their goal is to perform well, not to make a lot of money. Money is always the by-product of skill. It takes time to master music. Great musicians become artists by adding a part of themselves to the science of music.

(Now reread this paragraph and replace the word *music* with the words *trading and investing,* and replace the word *musicians* with the words *financial traders and investors.*)

YOUR BUSINESS PLAN

Objective: Get profitable. Design a business plan for your trading and investing business. This is an essential step. Every great company has a business plan. You are no different. Your business plan should be very specific. Following are seven issues and topics to address:

1. **Capital, equity drawdown, and margin.** Plan out how you will fund this new trading business. Be sure to allow for all living expenses necessary to maintain your current lifestyle while trading. Itemize both personal expenses and business operating expenses in great detail to determine your estimated monthly overhead. Determine what dollar amount you will start off with in your active trading account. Also, will you use margin, and, if so, how will you limit your risk? Establish how much equity drawdown (trading losses) will be acceptable before you stop trading and reevaluate your approach to the market.

2. **Business and office setup.** Outline exactly what you want your business to look like. List everything you will need, from computers to chairs. Then calculate what the cost of all these items will be and allocate a portion of your start-up capital for that purpose.

   Where will you conduct business? Is this going to be a home-based venture, or will you be operating from an outside office? What will your office space cost, and will you be operating on a full-time or part-time basis? Plus, have you decided what markets you will trade and what brokerage house you will use to execute your trades? Determine in advance what the commission cost of your trades will be.

   And, most importantly, select a proven trading system that you feel comfortable with and truly believe in. This trading system should suit your psychological approach and your personality.

3. **Legal and financial concerns.** If you are going to be a full-time trader, will you incorporate or be a limited partnership or sole proprietor? Will you open a separate bank account for this purpose? If you are managing your own investments, to which accounts will you be giving your attention? With regard to taxes, be familiar with any tax laws

DO NOT DISTURB!

This can be a somewhat delicate topic—keeping well meaning co-workers, family members, and phone solicitors "out of your hair." Trading and financial investing success cannot be attained without your undivided attention and concentration. Here's your plan of action:

1. Find a room in your house or office with a door that you can close and make that your "work room."
2. Communicate to your family and/or co-workers that you are under no circumstances to be interrupted while you are working (or studying). This communication should be clear and firm.
3. Hang a "Do Not Disturb" door sign from now on while trading and studying.
4. Do not answer the phone while working on your trading and investing. Use an answering machine or answering service. Get caller ID so you can screen out unnecessary calls.

---

that relate to your trading and investing. Who will prepare your tax returns, and can they counsel you on how to structure your business? Be prepared for an Internal Revenue tax audit, since random audits are always a possibility.

4. **Education.** Plan to learn your selected trading system's entries and exits by paper-trading until you know the system inside and out. Decide how long to paper-trade before going live.

Once you've started trading real dollars with your system, be true to this system and follow it to the letter. During periods of equity drawdown, do not be quick to abandon your chosen system. It's like a marriage. Use great caution before switching from one system to another. If the system is genuinely suited to you, stick with it.

Next, how will you develop the skills to become consistently profitable? Can you obtain training and education to speed you along on the path of profitability by developing the proper trading skills you will need for your selected trading system?

Then, find a mentor to whom you can look for support, guidance, and direction. This should be someone that you respect and admire and that you feel has in the past and will in the future continue to teach you what is important about trading and/or life.

Finally, you may need periodic coaching to help you stay on track with your trading system and business plan. Try to set up some coaching support in advance for those times when you feel that you are not achieving the goals set out in your business plan. You may want to contact TradersCoach.com to find out more about available coaching consultation packages.

5. **Goals and expectations.** Ask yourself: "What do I hope to accomplish by setting up this new business?"

Financial freedom? An independent and entrepreneurial work environment? Maybe it's as simple as being able to do what you love to do. Or do you just want to be in the driver's seat when it comes to your investments, instead of relying on a broker. The important thing is for you to look inside yourself and to find out what your answer to this question is. It will be revealing and will help you determine if you are pursuing this road for the right reasons.

Other important questions to ask are:

"Where do I want my trading and investing to be in six months, one year, and five years from now?"

"How much net revenue do I expect to generate on a monthly and yearly basis?"

"Do I anticipate continuing with this business indefinitely if it is everything I am hoping it will be—or is this a short-term stepping stone to something else?"

"If this is a short-term stepping stone, what is the next step after a successful trading and investing business?"

"If I am trading on a part-time basis, do I plan to leave my current employment and, if so, when?"

By clarifying your goals on paper you are more likely to make them into a successful reality. You can also see in black and white if your goals and expectations are realistic and can plan more effectively to overcome any obstacles that might present themselves when you start to sketch in the details.

6. **Record keeping and measuring progress.** Essential to your success is thorough and accurate record keeping. Be sure to record each trade's activity on a trade posting card to determine profitability. It is important to have your trades on paper to prevent confusion should your computer system go down. A handwritten card system also enables you to quickly jot down any feelings or thoughts that occur during the trading day. This will help you to work on your trading psychology.

Then maintain a running trade ledger of all trades to evaluate your profitability on a weekly, monthly, and annual basis. Look for any strengths or weaknesses that appear to correspond to the time of day, week, or year or the type of trade being executed. Where are you most profitable, and where are you least profitable?

ESSENTIAL STATISTICS TO TRACK

1. Average winning trade
2. Average losing trade
3. Win ratio and payoff ratio
4. Ratio of commission cost to profit earned
5. Margin liabilities
6. Percent of profit and loss

It is beneficial to have your system in place before you begin to make live trades. Trading is a fast-paced business, and your record keeping can easily get away from you if it is not considered a priority.

You may want to consider The Trader's Assistant record-keeping system by TradersCoach.com. For more information, see Appendix D at the back of this book.

7. **Your new trading and investing job.** Consider yourself an employee of this new company and map out what your new job will be like. Specify how many days a week you will work, how many hours per day, whether you will take a vacation, how you will manage sick days, and what kind of performance reviews there will be and when they will take place. How will you create accountability? Last but not least, are there retirement benefits and health care benefits in place?

Don't neglect doing a business plan. If you don't do one or feel it is not necessary, think again. It is vital. Another added benefit to this exercise is that you are instilling within yourself the discipline needed to succeed, much like the discipline and preparation needed before making a trade! It is all connected.

CHAPTER 8

Selecting a Financial Market

C hoosing the best market(s) for you to trade or invest in may take some time. Eventually, you will settle on your favorites and will develop an understanding of the unique characteristics of these markets. This will give you an edge in effectively implementing your trading and investing system to generate greater profits. If you are new to the markets, this chapter is designed to give you an overview and head start on what direction to go in.

SELECTING A MARKET

Selecting a market to trade is a combination of several factors such as:

- Market cycle
- Volatility
- Liquidity
- Trading or investment account value
- Market price
- Time frame you want to trade
- Your skill level
- How much time you have to monitor the markets

Here are six items to consider prior to choosing a market:

1. *Dollar size of your trading account.* Some markets may be too expensive for you even to consider trading. You may not be able to afford the market, or you cannot trade it and still maintain effective risk control. Sometimes by choosing a lower time frame, you can still maintain effective risk control.

2. *Amount of time you have to monitor the markets.* Different trading styles require different time obligations. If you day trade, then you need to be available to watch and monitor your trading all day during market hours. However, if you are position trading, then you only need to monitor the markets in the evening. Position trading is great for people who work during the day.

3. *The time frame you want to use.* If you are a day trader, you will choose an intraday time frame to trade; if you are a position trader, you will choose a daily time frame; and if you are an investor or long-term trader, you will choose weekly and monthly time frames. Choosing the best time frame is a combination of your trading account size, your risk control approach, and your personal preferences.

4. *Your overall knowledge of the markets.* As you gain experience and knowledge about the financial markets, you will expand your trading and investing possibilities. For example, most novice students start out with the stock market, but as they learn about other markets, such as options and futures, they may branch out to new areas.

5. *Your trading and investing skill level.* Don't confuse this with your overall market knowledge. This topic deals specifically with your trading and investing ability. Some markets require a higher level of skill due to their higher level of volatility or movement. You need to work with markets with which your skill level is compatible.

6. *Your personal preference.* Simply stated, what markets do you like best? Some students who are farmers may focus their trading on the commodities markets, such as the grain markets, while others on Wall Street may want to focus their trading and investing on the stock market.

TABLE OF MARKETS

The information in Table 8.1 (on pages 50–51) is subject to change at any time and is for educational purposes only. Check with your commodities broker for current commodity specifications before trading.

GREAT DAY TRADING MARKETS

- S&P e-mini (ES) futures market
- S&P futures market
- NASDAQ e-mini (NQ) futures market

These markets are liquid, competitive, fun, and fast and exhibit good intraday trends. I also have enjoyed trading the NASDAQ QQQQ (formerly known as the QQQ) and the DIA (Dow Diamonds) indexes.

The futures markets are set up for speculating, and the stock markets are set up for investing. Short-term traders are speculating. However, a valid argument is that there are more opportunities in the stock market because there are more stocks than futures markets.

You decide which markets are best for you. The e-mini markets are electronic, with fast fills, which are great for day trading. Also, with an e-mini market you can buy more contracts than the regular contract of that market, which can be advantageous, especially when applying "scaling-out" techniques that require multiple contracts. In addition, the e-mini markets can be traded with smaller trading accounts while still operating within proper money management risk controls and trade size.

ATTENTION OPTION TRADERS

If you trade options, you will apply the ART principles to the chart of the underlying asset. You will be trading the option of that underlying asset.

There are many ways to trade options, but ART focuses on buying deep in-the-money call options to go long and buying deep in-the-money put options to go short. Some traders like to sell options, but here we'll work on how you can use ART to trade options.

The key in trading options short term is to be sure you are trading the most liquid contract month and choose a "strike price" that yields a delta as close to 1:1 as possible. A delta of 1:1 means that when the underlying asset changes price, the premium price of that option also changes by the same amount.

To achieve this, you need to trade an option that is in-the-money enough to obtain as close as possible to a 1:1 delta. This eliminates the time value of the option so you can make an equal amount on the option as the underlying asset when it changes price. Don't forget, not only is the 1:1 delta important, but so is choosing the option with sufficient liquidity to achieve adequate fills quickly when entering and exiting short-term trades.

TABLE 8.1 Table of Markets

	Stocks	Options	Futures	Forex	Bonds	Mutual Funds
Market Types	Equities	Stocks, futures, index	Commodity futures, financial futures	Pairs and cross-markets	Debt	Equities, debt
Major Market Exchanges	New York Stock Exchange (NYSE), Nasdaq, American Stock Exchange (AMEX), Boston Stock Exchange (BSE), worldwide exchanges	Chicago Board Options Exchange (CBOE)	Chicago Mercantile Exchange (CME), New York Futures Exchange (NYFE), New York Mercantile Exchange (NYMEX), Chicago Board of Trade (CBOT), International Monetary Market (IMM), Minneapolis Grain Exchange (MGEX), Chicago Climate Exchange (CCX)	CME, banks	Over-the-counter, bond dealers	Open-end fund, exchange-traded funds, equity funds

Suggested Markets	All liquid markets, large-cap, mid-cap, small-cap	Calls, puts, spreads, hedging	All liquid markets, e-minis	AUD/USD, GBP/USD, USD/CAD, EUR/USD	Short-term debt, long-term debt	Equity income, balanced sector
Increments of Movement	Decimals	Decimals and quarter points	Ticks	PIP (percentage in point)		NAV (net asset value)
Suggested Experience Levels	Master Intermediate Novice	Master Intermediate	Master Intermediate	Master Intermediate	Master Intermediate	Master Intermediate Novice
Suggested Time Frames	Day trader Position Investor	Day trader Position Investor	Position Investor	Day trader Position Investor	Position Investor	Position Investor
Volume and Liquidity	Best during normal market hours	Best during normal market hours	Best during normal market hours	Long trading hours (except on weekends)	Best during normal market hours	Best during normal market hours
Notes	Index (ETF), QQQQ, DIA	Wide bid/ask make day trading difficult	Day trade: S&P e-mini and Nasdaq e-mini	No commissions but brokers make $ on spreads, 24-hour market	Long-term and short-term trading	"Pro-funds" are best for active mutual fund trading

Trading options in this way is acceptable and allows you to trade with more leverage than buying the underlying asset outright. In some cases, trading with options can help you increase your trade size, allowing you to implement scaling techniques.

USING STOCK SECTORS AND GROUPS TO BETTER YOUR ODDS

This is for equity traders and stock option traders. There are two approaches you can use to decide what stocks to trade. One is called a top-down approach, and the other is called a down-up approach. Here are the differences:

1. Top-down approach:
   a. Sector
   b. Group
   c. Individual

   In using this approach, you start the analysis at the sector level and work your way downward to individual stocks. Traders using this approach first look at the stock sector charts. Then they analyze the groups, and then pick the best individual stocks to trade, thus the name "top-down approach."

   You can use this approach by looking for sectors that have been sleepy for awhile. Then look at the most sleepy stock groups within that sector. Then, choose the best or longest-sleeping individual stock in that group and use the Pyramid Trading Point to enter.

   Another way to use this top-down approach would be to look for the strongest trending sector, up or down. Then wait for an ART Reversal to form and find the best group in the sector. Finally, identify the best individual stock that has also formed the pattern you are looking for.

   Maybe you want to look for a strong trend and a pullback, and then a reversal pattern back in the direction of the trend. Or you may want to go short off the ART Reversal and trade the correction. There are different patterns to look for, depending on how you want to trade and what makes you comfortable.

2. Down-up approach:
   a. Individual
   b. Group
   c. Sector

In this approach you will find the individual stock first and then analyze the group and finally the sector to see how the stock is behaving in relation to its peers. This can be helpful when you are getting a signal to go long on an individual stock, but the volume is a bit low and you are wondering why.

If you look at the group and it is in a downtrend, and your individual stock is generating a long position on low volume with no positive news out, then I might question going long. Again, if it is in play by either momentum traders or position traders, you will see significant volume on the time frame you are trading. The more volume, the more players are participating.

This down-up approach has saved me many times from going into the market when it is not ready to move. It will show you when the market is being manipulated on low volume by market makers. Real trends take "outside paper" coming from off the floor to move prices significantly.

Many traders worldwide need to be participating for a significant trend to develop. Significant trends occur when traders from many different time frames are participating in the trend.

When using the ART top-down or down-up approach, you can get an idea of who is involved in that stock you are about to trade. If the sector is not performing well, chances are that long-term investors are not buying now. They may be holding or waiting to buy, but they are most likely not buying a downtrending sector or group. It is possible that they have sold their positions already.

This is why bullish trading swings remain small until sectors turn around. Without the investor group's money to add buoyancy to a stock in a poor sector, smaller short-term traders can then cause these stocks to sell off more dramatically by shorting the stock, especially if the significant money is not buying the stock at that time.

By keeping trading techniques and ideas as simple as possible, you can quickly confirm a trade without getting bogged down with too much information. When I look at groups or sectors, it does not take me more than a few minutes and sometimes less to confirm a signal.

It needs to be that quick or you will never use it, especially if you are trading intraday. You can use intraday charts for groups and sectors, too, if you have intraday data for them.

If you are a scalper or trading under 10 minutes, it becomes impractical to view groups and sectors and stay focused on that short time frame. Activity in groups and sectors probably won't be of much help under a 15-minute time frame and is best used for 60-minute, daily, and weekly charts.

CHAPTER 9

Selecting a Time Frame

When we talk about time frames, we are discussing the interval of time it takes for one "price bar" to open and close on a chart. You will need to know how to select the best time frames in order to be successful. There is an art to this, and as you gain experience, you will develop your own style of selecting time frames. To start, based on your ART Profile from Chapter 6, you will already know whether your frequency identifies you as a day trader, position trader, or investor.

SELECTING A TIME FRAME

Selecting a time frame to trade is a combination of several factors such as:

- Market cycle
- Volatility
- Liquidity
- Trading or investment account value
- Market price
- Market you want to trade
- Your skill level
- How much time you have to monitor the markets

Based on your ART Profile, the following is a ballpark for you to work with when selecting time frames:

- Day trader—uses one- to five-minute-interval charts.
- Position trader—uses daily, weekly, and 60-minute-interval charts.
- Investor—uses weekly, monthly, and yearly interval charts.

Determine Market Cycle

When using the ART trading software, look to see if the time frame you are considering is currently:

- In a trend
- In a consolidation
- Just breaking out of a consolidation
- In a correction

Obviously, you do not want to jump into a mature trend that is near exhaustion, and you don't want to be whipsawed during a correction phase.

One technique is to look for a time frame that has been consolidated for an extended period of time. Then watch for a new breakout trend to occur.

FOUR MARKET CYCLES

1. Trending: A market that is moving consistently in one direction, up or down.
2. Consolidating: Also known as a *bracketing market,* this is when the market is stuck in a price range between an identifiable "resistance" and "support" level. On a chart, it will look like a sideways horizontal line.
3. Breaking out of a consolidation: A sharp change in price movement after the market has been consolidating for at least 20 price bars.
4. Corrective: A short, sharp reverse in prices during a longer market trend.

Determine Volatility

Choose a time frame where you do not get stopped out often when the market is trending. This is accomplished by watching a variety of time frames of the same market. This way, you can see which one has been the most stable for your style of trading.

Your trading account size and the price of the market you want to trade will determine what time frame you can trade, while maintaining proper risk control. This does not mean you should trade that market and time frame if the market cycle and volatility are not supportive to your style of trading.

Holding Trades Overnight and Assuming Overnight Risk

When trading a 15-minute time frame, your stop loss and position size will be based on the 15-minute time frame. But let's say you are 5 minutes from the close of the day and the trade is profitable, and much more profit is possible if you hold the trade overnight based on the 15-minute chart. As soon as you consider holding a trade overnight, you must consider the "rules of engagement."

"RULES OF ENGAGEMENT" FOR OVERNIGHT TRADES

1. The trade must currently be profitable.
2. The 15-minute chart must indicate a solid trend in place.
3. You must set a new stop loss based on the daily chart.
4. Reduce trade size so that risk remains no more than 2 percent of your trading account (based on the new adjusted stop from the daily chart).
5. Monitor the trade at the opening bell the next morning.

These same rules apply when going from a 5-minute chart to a 15-minute chart. Trade size must be adjusted.

Knowing about Fundamentals

As a general rule of thumb, the lower (or faster) a time frame you choose to trade, the less you need to know about the company in terms of fundamentals and news.

If you're a long-term investor, you should know a lot about the company you are about to buy, such as management's track record, earnings, debts, P/E (price-to-earnings ratio), and multiples for that sector or group. Basically, you need to know the fundamentals of the company. If you are a day trader or a market "scalper," you will have little interest in fundamentals. You'll focus only on short-term technical charts and momentum.

You may use fundamentals to find markets to trade and then use the ART software to tell you when to enter and exit that market.

Use Caution When Day Trading

The ART techniques can be used on any time frame, including intraday trading, otherwise known as day trading. When choosing the intraday time frame you want to trade, you must keep the following points in mind:

- The shorter the time frame, the more trading skill is required.
- Short one- to five-minute time frames are especially influenced by traders of higher time frames. Trading systems can experience difficulties due to trading activity outside their chosen time frame, which the trading system cannot see or measure. You may experience drawdown when the realities of higher time frames affect the realities of the time frame you have chosen to trade.
- While your system may accurately indicate the realities of the time frame you are trading, you may still experience a loss from stronger realities of another time frame. This is an argument for trading in alignment with the Higher Time Frame Filter (see "Advanced Techniques" in Part V).
- Or you may just accept this type of drawdown, using proper risk control. You would then trade through it without having to be preoccupied with many different time frames.

CHAPTER 10

Selecting an ART Platform, Broker, and Data Feed

W hen it's time to select your ART platform, broker and data provider, you have a variety to choose from. See Tables 10.1 through 10.3. Study the information in this chapter carefully and contact each of the vendors directly so that you obtain the best combination of services for your current needs.

ART Platforms

Make sure your ART platform supports the market, data feed, and broker you plan to use. They must all be compatible and work together. For example, if you decide to trade the FOREX, which is specialized, be sure that the ART platform you select has access to this market. Remember, the information stated in this book is current as of today. There may be additional platforms added in the future. For the most current information go online to www.TradersCoach.com.

Brokers

Do your research and match your needs to the broker you select. Each of the brokers listed have different levels of customer service, available markets and service fees. For example, Interactive Brokers is for very experienced traders. This means that they provide very little customer service support. You may even be required to show statements proving that you have already completed 100 trades. Unless you are very experienced, go with TradeStation or TD AMERITRADE. Remember, do your homework before opening an account.

Data Feeds

Depending on your current situation, you may be able to get free data from your broker, if you are an active trader. Otherwise there are a number of independent data providers for you to choose from, eSignal being one of the very best.

TABLE 10.1   Table of ART Platforms

	Phone Numbers, Web Site, and E-Mail Contact Information	Markets Available	Compatible Brokers and Data Feeds Include But Are Not Limited To The Following
TradeStation Securities	800-292-3476 954-652-7407 www.tradestation.com	All markets	Compatible with: TradeStation Securities & Data Feed IQ Feed (DTN Markets) Data Feed
QuoteTracker (TD Ameritrade Securities)	www.quotetracker.com	Stocks Mutual funds Options Bonds	Compatible with: TD Ameritrade Securities & Data Feed
eSignal (Data Feed)	800-815-8256 512-723-1765 www.esignal.com	All markets	Compatible with: Interactive Brokers GAIN Capital MB Trading OptionsXpress
NinjaTrader	www.ninjatrader.com	All markets	Compatible with: Interactive Brokers TD Ameritrade GAIN Capital MB Trading Mirus Futures eSignal Data Open Tick Data DTN.IQ Data

This information is subject to change at any time and is for educational purposes only.

TABLE 10.2 Table of Online Brokers

	TD Ameritrade	TradeStation	Interactive Brokers
Toll-Free Phone	800-454-9272	800-292-3476	877-442-2757
Web Site	www.tdameritrade.com	www.tradestation.com	www.interactivebrokers.com
Direct-Dial Phone	402-970-5805	954-652-7407	312-542-6901
Markets Available from Broker	Stocks Mutual funds Options Bonds	All markets	All markets
Minimum Account to Open	$2,000 USD	$5,000 USD	$10,000 USD
Margin Rate	11%	8%	8%
Compatible with ART Software	Yes (Quotracker provides free data)	Yes (TradeStation provides free data on all markets for active clients)	Yes For experienced traders only (get free data when linked to NinjaTrader or eSignal Platforms for active clients)
	$ Cost/Trade	**$ Cost/Trade**	**$ Cost/Trade**
Stocks	$10/Trade	.006/Share	.005/Share
Options	$1/Contract	$1/Contract	$1/Contract
Futures	N/A	$1/Contract	$1/Contract

This information is subject to change at any time and is for educational purposes only.

TABLE 10.3 Table of Live Data Feeds

	eSignal	TradeStation	NinjaTrader
Toll-Free Phone	800-815-8256	800-292-3476	N/A
Website	www.esignal.com	www.tradestation.com	www.ninjatrader.com
Direct-Dial Phone	512-723-1765	954-652-7407	N/A
Includes Charting Platform	Yes	Yes	Yes (connects to many third-party data sources and brokers)
Stocks	Yes	Yes	Yes
Options	Yes	Yes	Yes
Futures	Yes	Yes	Yes
Forex	Yes	Yes	Yes
Bonds	Yes	Yes	Yes
Compatible with ART Software	Yes	Yes	Yes

This information is subject to change at any time and is for educational purposes only.

CHAPTER 11

Psychology and the Trader's Mind-Set

D eveloping the trader's mind-set is a must for trading (and investing) success, and this can take some time. It is not an area where you can take a shortcut or learn a formula. It can be developed only by actually trading and from the experiences you will gain from trading. We will help guide you toward developing the trader's mind-set. We'll also help you manage the emotions associated with account drawdowns, losses, and profits (yes, profits and winning can actually cause stress!).

100 TRADERS AND INVESTORS—EACH IS UNIQUE

If you show the same successful financial approach to 100 different people, no two of them will use it in exactly the same way. Why? Because each individual has a unique belief system, and those beliefs will determine his or her personal style.

Even with a profitable and proven approach, many traders and investors will fail. If they do not have the proper belief system to trade, they will lose. In other words, they lack the trader's mind-set.

SELF-AWARENESS

When you encounter a psychological issue, it is best to recognize the issue and not deny it. To eliminate psychological obstacles, you must first become aware of the obstacles and the issues causing them. This requires self-awareness.

In psychoanalysis a psychologist or psychotherapist helps the client first see the problem. The reason this process can take so long, perhaps even years, is that individuals will have varying levels of denial. After they see the problems, they must take responsibility for them. There is little room for denial when it comes to financial issues—if you want to be consistently profitable.

15 COMMON DESTRUCTIVE PSYCHOLOGICAL TRADING ISSUES AND THEIR CAUSES

1. *Fear of being stopped out or of taking a loss.* The usual reason for this is that the trader fears failure and feels like he or she cannot take another loss. The trader's ego is at stake.

2. *Getting out of trades too early.* The trader relieves anxiety by closing a position. He has a fear of the position's reversing and then feeling let down or a need for instant gratification.

3. *Wishing and hoping.* The trader does not want to take control or take responsibility for the trade or has an inability to accept the present reality of the marketplace.

4. *Anger after a losing trade.* The trader has the feeling of being a victim of the markets, unrealistic expectations, or caring too much about a specific trade. He ties his self-worth to his success in the markets or needs approval from the markets.

5. *Trading with money you cannot afford to lose or trading with borrowed money.* The trader feels that this is his last hope at success and is trying to be successful at something. He has a fear of losing his chance at opportunity, no discipline, greed, or desperation.

6. *Adding on to a losing position (doubling down).* The trader does not want to admit his trade is wrong and is hoping it will come back. His ego is at stake.

7. *Compulsive trading.* The trader is drawn to the excitement of the markets. Addiction and gambling issues are present. He needs to feel he is always in the game and has difficulty when not trading, such as on weekends. He is obsessed with trading.

8. *Excessive joy after a winning trade.* The trader ties his self-worth to the markets, feeling unrealistically "in control" of the markets.

9. *Stagnant or poor trading account profits—limiting profits.* The trader feels that he doesn't deserve to be successful, that he doesn't deserve money or profits. There are usually psychological issues such as poor self-esteem.

10. *Not following your trading system.* The trader doesn't believe it really works. He did not test it well. It does not match his personality. He wants more excitement in his trading. He doesn't trust his own ability to choose a successful system.

11. *Overthinking the trade, second-guessing your trading.* The trader has a fear of loss or being wrong. He has a perfectionist personality, wanting a sure thing where sure things don't exist. He does not understand that loss is a part of trading, and the outcome of each trade is unknown. He does not accept that there is risk in trading and does not accept the unknown. He is afraid to pull the trigger.

12. *Not trading the correct trade size.* The trader is dreaming that the trade will be only profitable and not fully recognizing the risk or understanding the importance of money management. He refuses to take responsibility for managing his risk or is too lazy to calculate proper trade size.

13. *Trading too much.* The trader has a need to conquer the market. Greed. Trying to get even with the market for a previous loss. The excitement of trading (similar to Number 7, Compulsive Trading).

14. *Afraid to Trade.* The trader has no trading system in place. He is not comfortable with risk and the unknown and has a fear of total loss, fear of ridicule, need for control, and no confidence in his trading system or himself.

15. *Irritable after the trading day.* The trader is on an emotional roller coaster due to anger, fear, and greed, putting too much attention on trading results and not enough on the process and learning the skill of trading. He is focusing on the money too much and has unrealistic trading expectations.

These are by no means all the psychological issues but some of the most common. They usually center on the fact that, for one reason or another, the trader is not following his chosen trading approach or system.

Your goal is to maintain an even keel. Your winning trades and losing trades should not affect you. Obviously, you are trading better when you are winning, but emotionally you should strive to maintain an even balance regarding wins and losses.

It will happen when it happens. It cannot be forced. When you achieve this level of mental ability, it will come after working long and hard on your weaknesses, but will come without your knowing it. It usually happens when you least expect it.

HERE IS WHAT YOU'LL FEEL AFTER ACQUIRING THE TRADER'S MIND-SET

1. Not caring about the money.
2. Acceptance of the risk in trading and investing.
3. Winning and losing trades accepted equally from an emotional standpoint.
4. Enjoyment of the process.
5. No feeling of being victimized by the markets.
6. Always looking to improve skills.
7. Trading and investing account profits now accumulating and flowing in as skills improve.
8. Opened-minded, keeping opinions to a minimum.
9. No anger.
10. Learning from every trade or position.
11. Using one chosen approach or system and not being influenced by the market or other traders.
12. No need to conquer or control the "market."
13. Feeling confident and feeling in control.
14. A sense of not forcing the markets.
15. Trading with money you can afford to risk.
16. Taking full responsibility for all trading results.
17. Sense of calmness when trading.
18. Ability to focus on the present reality.
19. Not caring which way the market breaks or moves.
20. Aligning trades in the direction of the market, flowing with the market.

When you can read the trader's mind-set list and genuinely say "that's me," you have arrived!

One important key in acquiring the trader's mind-set is to create a sense of balance in your trading and in your life. Each of us is able to reduce trading stress in different ways and you will need to find what works best for you. By reducing stress on a daily basis you are one step closer to the trader's mind-set.

CHAPTER 12

Artistic Simplicity

The Applied Reality Trading system is designed to help you trade in the present moment and enable you to focus on the reality of the marketplace as it is unfolding. ART intentionally does not use indicators that distort the truths of the market. The ART approach is much like a lie detector, which filters out fact from fiction.

In reality, you don't know how the market will respond to news, earnings, world events, economic events, and so on. In fact, at times you won't know if the earnings numbers are the truth. Some major companies "alter" their numbers. Even news commentators love to tell the public stories about why this stock dropped and another went up. Sometimes they are right, and sometimes they don't have a clue. And when they are right, it is usually in hindsight when the stock has already moved, which has no value for you.

IT IS POSSIBLE TO RECEIVE TOO MUCH INFORMATION

Too much information can lead to confusion, frustration, lack of confidence, and poor trading. Eliminate the extra noise created by the media and indicators and seek the truth of the markets to become a successful trader. Eliminate opinions about the market when you trade. Avoid information overload.

SIMPLIFY AND FLOW WITH THE MARKET

Follow the markets and don't try to figure out why they are moving, just move along with them. You can do this if you keep your mind clear and focus on the present reality.

Much like when you play your best game of tennis, golf, or basketball, you will notice that it just happened: everything was in sync, you were focused and in the zone. That is the state you want to be in when you are trading. Applied Reality Trading helps you get in this focused zone where everything is in harmony. You will learn how to simplify and flow with the market.

GUIDELINES TO SIMPLIFY YOUR TRADING AND INVESTING

1. Don't rely on your broker for trading advice.
2. Remember, trading and investing is a skill—be patient.
3. Continually practice the art of focusing on the present moment (it's hard to do). Don't think about yesterday or tomorrow—focus on the now.
4. Manually keep excellent records of all your transactions.
5. Eliminate negative distractions while working.
6. Enjoy the process.
7. Don't listen to financial news during business hours.
8. Use one trading and financial approach and follow it consistently.
9. Don't have lofty and unrealistic expectations.
10. Focus on your skills when you are not meeting your performance expectations.
11. Don't read newspapers for trading information.
12. If you feel sick, don't trade until you feel better.
13. If you feel emotionally upset, don't trade until you are more stable.
14. If you have a specific problem that is distracting you, don't trade.
15. Resist the temptation to form opinions about each trade.
16. Eliminate any opinions you may have about the market.
17. Keep your mind clear and focused.

The goal is to create a clear mind, free of distractions and opinions. The markets are a living system, much like humans are, and as a result are unpredictable. The only way you can successfully profit in the markets is to stop trying to predict the unpredictable. Like a tail on a dog, just follow the markets. When they go up, go with them. When they go down, go with them. When they are doing nothing, do nothing.

REDUCING STRESS AND CREATING BALANCE

Here are some ideas to get you started in reducing stress and creating harmony and balance:

- Consider getting a dog (or bird, or cat, or fish or any pet).
- Walk the dog.
- Go outside, away from the office, and get some fresh air.
- Do some gardening.
- Go out for a romantic dinner.
- Get a massage, manicure, or pedicure.
- Go to the gym; start an exercise program.
- Soak up some sunshine—lie in the sun or sit outside; if you live in a cloudy climate, visit a sunny destination.
- Set up a tennis date (or any team sport).
- Go for a dip in the Jacuzzi or take a hot bath.
- Enjoy your favorite hobby.
- Start a new hobby.
- Go on vacation—change your scenery—visit a sunny destination.
- Play your favorite game (e.g., checkers, chess, canasta, poker, computer games).
- Start eating healthier; drink more water.
- Hug your kids.
- Go for a bicycle ride or run on a new route you haven't tried before.
- Donate time or money to a favorite organization or cause.
- Walk on the beach.
- Do yoga or meditation.
- Read a good book.
- Go out to a movie (instead of renting one at home).

(*continued*)

- Throw a party at your house; entertain.
- Call up an old friend.
- Make a new friend.
- Enjoy the nature around you—watch an eagle flying overhead, the clouds, a sunset or a sunrise, the ocean waves, a sandy beach.
- Stop to smell the roses.

Finding harmony and balance is a personal choice. It is crucial that you don't get obsessed with your trading and finances 24 hours a day, 7 days a week. Having passion for your work is a wonderful thing as long as you maintain balance with the rest of your life.

TRADING ERRORS, ARTISTIC BLOCKS, AND OVERCOMING THEM

Every great artist encounters periods where they hit a "brick wall"—their creativity is blocked and they just get stuck. As traders and investors we face the same challenges from time to time, and there are ways we can get back on track.

Here are a few of the ways to get back on track:

1. Take time off and relax; then, when you are fresh, try again.
2. Before sleeping, ask yourself a question regarding your "brick wall"; then, while you're sleeping, let your subconscious mind work on it.
3. Try focusing on your problem at different times of the day or evening.

CHAPTER 13

The Art of Paper-Trading

I t is imperative first to be profitable when paper-trading before trading with real money. Paper-trading is an art in which you design a profitable approach and practice until it becomes second nature.

While paper-trading will not have the same psychological "feel" as trading with real money, it is a useful way to practice your skills in a stress-free environment so that you can focus on your financial approach and rules. Paper-trading gives you time to hone your skills without losing money.

EVERY FINANCIAL MARKET IS A CHAMPIONSHIP ARENA

Short-term trading is a zero-sum game. When you enter any financial market, you will be competing against some very skilled professional traders. If you enter the market as a novice, you will be competing against traders who have more skill and more experience. To give yourself a fighting chance, you need to enter the markets as skilled as possible. Anything less will make it hard for you to succeed in trading.

Develop your trading skills with paper-trading, which allows you to practice without the pressure of competing against others. If you cannot be profitable paper-trading, then you most likely will not be profitable trading with real money!

It is sometimes said that paper-trading is useless because you won't "feel" the psychological emotions that are experienced when trading with real money. I strongly disagree with this. As a matter of fact, you may find that, surprisingly enough, paper-trading can create a very similar emotional roller coaster as trading with real money, especially if you approach paper-trading with the same dedication that you approach trading with real money.

The deeper psychological and emotional aspects can be worked on later, after you have developed your trading skills. It is better to have your trading approach developed first, and then work on developing your trading psychology.

Don't be impatient with your paper-trading. Allow yourself time to develop your trading skills and approach. This is time very well spent, so no shortcuts here.

1. **Design your trading rules.** In an experimental environment (not using real money), practice mixing and matching the ART signals to suit your style. These signals are the Primary Pyramid Trading Point, Minor Pyramid Trading Point, ART One-Bar Reversal, and ART Two-Bar Reversal. You will find Part IV and Part V of this book useful in designing your personal trading rules.

2. **Start to paper-trade.** Once you feel you know the ART system and you know how you want to trade it, start paper-trading on the time frame and market you plan to trade when using real money. Decide what markets you want to trade. Choose stocks, futures, forex, options, indexes, and so on. If you have the time to day trade, it is best for you to paper-trade your favorite market. Day trading will shorten your learning curve because you will trade more often and gain more experience for a given period of time. This is the time to practice mixing and matching the ART trading signals until you develop a recipe that fits your unique belief system! See if trend trading, scalping, scaling in, or scaling out suits you. Through trial and error in a safe paper-trading environment, you will be able to determine how you want to trade the ART program.

3. **Evaluate your performance.** Keep track of your paper-trading results and approach this as if you are trading with real money. Use The Trader's Assistant Record Keeping and Trade Posting System by TradersCoach.com to evaluate your trading.

4. **Group in lots of 25 trades.** Group your paper-trades in lots of 25 trades each, and calculate your profit/loss, average win/loss, largest win/loss, number of winning trades, and number of losing trades, number of consecutive winning and losing trades.

5. **Practice until profitable.** Analyze your trading results and make adjustments until you are profitable, and feel good about your trading.

6. **Three Lots of 25 Trades.** Before trading with real money, be sure you have at least three profitable consecutive lots of 25 trades each while paper-trading. And if you're a day trader, be sure to have spread your day trading over enough days, weeks, or even months to have experienced uptrending, downtrending, and bracketed markets. Spread out your paper-trading over several weeks or even months so you experience a wide variety of markets.

7. **Keep trading in lots of 25 trades.** When trading with real money, keep using the 25-trade lot size to analyze your profit/loss and the like and see how you are doing.

8. **Reevaluate your approach.** If you are not profitable trading with real money after trading one lot of 25 trades, stop trading and go back to paper-trading again. If you are again profitable paper-trading, then chances are your psychology is the problem and you may need some additional help from a trading coach to uncover your psychological sabotage issues. If your paper-trading is not profitable this time, then you may have just been lucky the first time when you paper-traded and did not paper-trade long enough to experience the different types of market cycles. Your trading approach needs to be adjusted. Until you have a qualified trading approach as proven through how you paper-trade, then you will not know if you problem lies in your trading approach or if your problem is with your psychology.

9. **Experiencing losses.** If you experience six consecutive losing trades or a drawdown of more than 15 percent, the market cycle or volatility on the market and time frame you are trading has probably changed. You must adapt quickly and effectively to these changes.

10. **During drawdown follow these steps:**
    - Stop trading with real money. Keep trading the same market and time frame and go back to paper-trading. Wait until you have 3 winning lots of 25 paper-trades before trading with real money again.
    - Change the settings on the ART trading software to see if that eliminates the losses you incurred in your recent drawdown. If so, paper-trade again to validate the new software settings.
    - Change time frames until you find the time frame that is working the best; you may still have to adjust your ART software settings.
    - Experiment with some advanced techniques in Part V of this book.

FIGHTER PILOTS AND FLIGHT SIMULATORS

There is a reason that fighter pilots are required to be successful in a flight simulator on the ground before they are permitted to take an F18 fighter jet into the air: The government doesn't want them to crash and burn and waste valuable tax dollars. Paper-trading is the same as a flight simulator: Make sure you know how to fly before you put your hard-earned dollars into the market.

PART III

Science and Math

CHAPTER 14

Calculating Proper Trade Size

M oney management principles in trading cannot be overemphasized. We work in the world of probabilities and risk and part of this topic was covered in Chapter 3, when we talked about stop-loss exits. Now we will focus on trade size.

Since the future is impossible to predict, you cannot predict the outcome of each new transaction. Therefore, you must prepare for the possibility of loss. You do this by controlling your *trade size*, which is also known as your *position size*. This means the number of shares (for stocks) or the number of contracts (for futures and options) that you buy or sell (sell short).

With the ART system you will know your entry and exit before you enter each trade. Knowing this information allows you to calculate your maximum trade size risk for every trade.

CONTROLLING RISK

When controlling risk, there are three variables you can control:

1. Entry (where to get in)
2. Exit (where to set your initial stop)
3. Trade size (in shares or contracts)

THE 2 PERCENT RISK RULE

Never risk more than 2 percent (of your overall trading account size) on any one trade. You must be able to incur a number of losses in a row; this is known as *drawdown*. Advanced traders, see "Important Note" below. That is the goal of money management, and it separates the pros from the novices. Proper money management enables you to stay in the game and avoid entirely losing or depleting your capital.

- Never risk more than 2 percent of your trading account (see note below) on any one trade:

$$\$ \text{ Account Size} \times 2\% = \$ \text{ Risk Amount}$$

Example: $25,000 Account

$$\$25,000 \times 2\% = \$500$$

- Use proper trade size formula on every trade:

$$\frac{\$ \text{ Risk Amount} - \text{Commission}}{\$ \text{ Difference between Entry and Stop}} = \begin{array}{l} \text{Trade Size in Shares} \\ \text{or Contracts} \end{array}$$

Example: $500 Risk Amount, $80 Commission, $1.50 Points of Risk

$$\frac{\$500 - \$80}{\$1.50} = 280 \text{ Shares}$$

IMPORTANT NOTE

Advanced traders and investors can benefit from risking more than 2 percent of their trading capital on each trade. The 2 percent figure is used here in order to protect you from the risk of ruin.

If you feel you are advanced and need to calculate the correct risk amount on your trade size, you will need to determine your win ratio and your payoff ratio. Once you do that, then refer to *A Trader's Money Management System*, John Wiley & Sons (2008). This book has the information needed to correctly identify the proper risk amount for each trade.

THE PSYCHOLOGY BEHIND TRADE SIZE

Implementing sound money management encompasses many techniques and skills. Failure to implement a proven money management program in your trading will leave you subject to a deadly risk-of-ruin exposure, leading to a probable equity bust.

When someone makes a huge killing in the market on a relatively small or average trading account, they most likely were not implementing sound money management. In cases such as this, they're more than likely exposed to obscene risk because of an abnormally large trade size. In this case, the trader or "gambler" may have gotten lucky, leading to a profit windfall. If they continue trading, probabilities indicate that it is just a matter of time before huge losses dwarf the wins.

Or, when someone tells me that they trade the same number of shares or contracts on every trade, I know they are not calculating their optimal trade size. If they were, then the trade size would change from time to time when trading.

In order to implement a money management program to reduce your risk exposure, you must first believe you need to implement this sort of program. Usually, this belief comes from having large losses that cause enough psychological pain that you want and need to change.

Novice traders tend to focus on the trade outcome as only winning and do not think about risk. Master traders focus on the risk and take a trade based on a "probable" favorable outcome. The psychology behind trade size begins when you believe and acknowledge that each trade's outcome is unknown when entering the trade. Believing this makes you ask yourself, "How much can I afford to lose on this trade and not fall prey to risk of ruin?"

When traders ask themselves this question, they will either adjust their trade size or tighten their stop loss before entering the trade. In most situations, the best method is to adjust your trade size and set your stop loss based on market dynamics.

During drawdown periods, risk control becomes important. Since master traders test their trading systems, they know the probabilities of how many consecutive losses they may incur.

YOU'RE RIGHT 60 PERCENT OF THE TIME

The idea behind money management is that, given enough time, even the best trading systems will be right only about 60 percent of the time. That means 40 percent of the time you will be wrong and have losing trades. For every 10 trades, you will lose an average of 4 times.

Even trading systems or certain trading setups with advertised higher rates of return nearing 80 percent usually fall back to a realistic 60 percent return when actually traded.

So, if you are losing 40 percent of the time, then you need to control risk. This is done through implementing stops and controlling position and trade size. You never really know which trades will be profitable. As a result, you have to control risk on every trade regardless of how sure you think the trade will be.

If you let your winners ride and cut your losses quickly, you can do very well with a 60 percent trading system win-to-loss ratio. In fact, with risk control, you can sustain multiple consecutive losses without devastating your trading account. Remember, master traders and investors continue to use effective risk control. Risk control is essential no matter what your skill level is.

GOING BUST!

Some folks can start and end their financial careers in just one month. By not controlling risk and by using improper trade size, you can go broke in no time. It usually happens like this: You begin trading, get five losses in a row, don't use proper position size, and don't cut your losses soon enough. After five devastating losses in a row, your trading capital is now too low to continue trading. It can happen that quickly!

TRADING DRAWDOWN

It is important that you are comfortable with your system and know that it is possible to have a losing streak of five losses. This is called *drawdown*. Knowing this prepares you to control risk and not abandon your chosen trading system when drawdown occurs. We are striving for a balanced growth in your equity curve over time.

OVERTRADING

If you feel out of control at the pace you are going, you are overtrading. You will know it by the feelings of anxiety generated by your trading getting out of control. Some traders may deny these feelings up to a point, but eventually it becomes so severe that it cannot be denied.

Another sign will be your profit and loss. If your losses are unusually large and your commissions are a large portion of your losses, you are probably overtrading. If you find this happening, slow down or even stop trading until you find out why you are suddenly overtrading. You may be angry at the markets or at someone, or trying to earn a fast buck from the markets. Take some time off and relax.

THE SCIENCE OF TECHNICAL ANALYSIS

Technical analysis and fundamental analysis are primarily used to analyze the financial markets. While technical analysis studies price relationships, patterns, and indicators, fundamental analysis studies a company's performance numbers, weather conditions for crops, news events, and other similar characteristics.

The ART software is purely technical analysis because it focuses on price and volume analysis. But the ART methodology can include picking markets from a variety of both technical and fundamental analysis concepts. This means that while, at times, you may select markets to trade or invest in using a fundamental analysis, actual trade entries and exits are purely done using ART technical analysis.

The number of indicators, oscillators, and information sources available today is astounding. The reality is that "less is more." If you allow yourself to be inundated with unnecessary information and clutter, you will be drawn further away from the "truths" of the market—price and volume. The key with ART is to keep your analysis as simple and as focused as possible.

Simplicity will be the secret to your success. The ART system will simplify your trading and add structure, which helps to lessen anxiety that can lead to emotional trading.

Whether you use technical analysis or fundamental analysis, you need to base your trading decisions on reality. By using the ART software you will be following the reality of the markets represented by price and volume. In ART, we base our entries and exits on technical analysis realities.

CHAPTER 15

Other Formulas and Recipes

As with almost anything, successful trading and investing generally starts with some form of mathematical formula, equation, or recipe. For example, most of us will agree that the equation $E = mc^2$ and the most famous scientist of all time, Albert Einstein, will be inexplicably connected for eternity. Or isn't it fantastic that the secret recipe for Mrs. Fields cookies is the cornerstone for an entire multibillion-dollar corporation?

The point is that formulas and recipes are valuable in developing any successful company or product. And they are equally important for you in creating your own successful financial plan.

If you are more the artistic type, math and science may not be a natural part of your thought process. But, once you get going, it will become second nature and will automatically integrate into your creative process of trading and investing.

In the last chapter we covered the formula used to determine trade (or position) size. Following are a few other formulas that you will find helpful in establishing a practical financial plan.

10 PERCENT RISK RULE

It is best that you actively trade with less than 10 percent of your total net worth. Even though you are using sound risk control, you can't remove the market risk involved in active trading. Examples of market risk are events such as price gaps that can happen instantly, in which stop-loss exits may not be able to limit your risk. There is also a world of financial news events that can create market risk, and these can occur without warning. Just to name a few, no one could have anticipated an event like the World Trade Center 9/11 tragedy or Hurricane Katrina in the United States. These devastating events have an instant impact on the markets.

6 PERCENT RISK RULE

Another guideline to follow is to keep your total active trading account risk under 6 percent. This means you can have three live trades simultaneously, each allowing a 2 percent risk per trade, provided that each of the trades is in a different sector of the market. By diversifying in this way, you ensure that you are not trading or investing too heavily in any one area of the market.

2 PERCENT PER SECTOR RISK RULE

Don't put all your eggs into one basket! Basically, be sure that you diversify your trades, allowing only a maximum of 2 percent risk on your total trading account in any one sector. This will help protect from events like the technology sector bust in the year 2000. By diversifying in this way, you are managing your risk—not eliminating it, but giving yourself more control over significant market events.

SCALING OUT 33 PERCENT

This is an advanced technique, which you will learn more about in Part V of this book. The short take on this technique is to scale out of 33 percent of your position when you see a sharp move in the market that gives you substantial quick profit. You then leave the remaining two thirds of the position in the market. This is an effective technique for alleviating anxiety and stress. The crucial part of this formula is to be sure you scale out only when the ART software gives you a signal to do so—you don't arbitrarily decide to exit the market for emotional reasons.

   These formulas and recipes are a starting point. You will no doubt determine your own formulas as you design a custom approach using the ART software. Remember, always try to break down your approach into quantifiable formulas and recipes so that you can compare apples to apples and test new strategies. In that way, you will design very clear trading and investing rules that will minimize emotional trading and investing. Instead of random and emotional entries and exits, you will have a mathematical and scientific plan.

THE TRADER'S ASSISTANT™

TradersCoach.com has developed the best trade-posting and record-keeping system on the market today. It is called The Trader's Assistant, and it enables you to calculate your largest winning trade, largest losing trade, average winning trade, average losing trade, commission, profit and loss, and so on. If you don't currently evaluate your trading to determine where you stand with regard to this data, you must implement a system now.

You can't "fix" your trading if you do not know what is wrong with it. The information in The Trader's Assistant will help you to identify areas of weakness and strength using your actual performance results. This system was designed to allow traders, at any time during the year, to look at an individual trade—there's a posting card where you record the results, including your thoughts, emotions, and stops.

The other benefit of The Trader's Assistant is that it gets you in the habit of manually recording your trades and "running the numbers." In this day and age of computers (and believe me, I love computers), everybody is automating everything. If you automate your trading results, you will never really feel it.

When using The Trader's Assistant at the end of each day, each week, each month, and each year, you will feel like you have been given a complete debriefing of your trading. You will also feel like you have put your trading under a microscope and analyzed it. Using this record-keeping system will quickly point out trading problems that you will not be able to deny. The numbers will tell you the truth about your trading.

You can get a complete copy of The Trader's Assistant posting cards and ledgers in the book *A Trader's Money Management System: How To Ensure Profit And Avoid The Risk Of Ruin*, John Wiley & Sons (2008). You'll also learn about the methodology behind this system.

CHAPTER 16

The Human Brain

The human brain is like a supercharged custom Dell computer with feelings. It is an impressive supervisory center of the nervous system that serves as the site for all human emotions, memory, self-awareness, and thought. It weighs only three pounds and is a remarkable thing!

Our brains consist of some 10 billion interconnected nerve cells with innumerable extensions. This interlacing of nerve fibers and their junctions allows a nerve impulse to follow any of a virtually unlimited number of pathways. The effect is to give us a seemingly infinite variety of responses to sensory input. In this chapter you will see how using your brain and understanding your brain can enable you to create greater financial success.

5 FACTORS THAT AFFECT HOW TRADING INPUT IS PROCESSED IN YOUR BRAIN

The pathway a brain chooses for a sensory impulse depends on many factors, including:

1. The particular brain's unique physical characteristics.
2. Temporary physical conditions such as fatigue or malnourishment.
3. Information previously implanted by experience and learning.
4. Intensity of the stimulus producing the impulse.
5. Current emotional states such as anger, fear, or sadness.

ANATOMY OF THE BRAIN

The cerebrum, occupying the topmost portion of the skull, is by far the largest sector of the brain. Split vertically into left and right hemispheres, it appears deeply fissured and grooved. Its upper surface, the cerebral cortex, contains most of the master controls of the body. The left half of the cerebrum controls the right side of the body; the right half controls the left side of the body.

The brain is working during both sleep and consciousness for our entire life. The ceaseless electrochemical activity in the brain generates brain waves that can be electronically detected and recorded. The adult human brain consumes 25 percent of the energy used by the body, while the developing brain of an infant consumes around 60 percent.

LEFT BRAIN AND RIGHT BRAIN

Our brain is made up of two halves, a left brain and a right brain. There is a big fold that goes from front to back in our brain, essentially dividing it into two distinct and separate parts—well, almost separate. They are connected to each other by a thick cable of nerves at the base of each brain. This sole link between the two giant processors is called the corpus callosum. Think of it as an ethernet cable or network connection between two incredibly fast and immensely powerful computer processors, each running different programs from the same sensory input.

Scientists are learning more about the nature of the left and right brain every day. They have learned that each side of the brain has strengths in certain areas (see left brain, right brain table), although the fact is that mental abilities are not entirely separated into the left and right cerebral hemispheres. Speech and language tend to be localized to specific areas in one hemisphere, but if one hemisphere is damaged at an early age, these functions can often be recovered in part or even in full by the other hemisphere.

> *... there appears to be two modes of thinking, verbal and nonverbal, represented rather separately in left and right hemispheres respectively and that our education system, as well as science in general, tends to neglect the nonverbal form of intellect. What it comes down to is that modern society discriminates against the right hemisphere of the brain ...*

—Roger Sperry (1973)
Nobel Prize winner (1981)

LEFT BRAIN, RIGHT BRAIN CHARACTERISTICS

Left Brain (Scientific)	Right Brain (Artistic)
Uses logic and planning	Uses feelings and emotions
Follows rules	Follows impulses
Uses words	Uses pictures
Identifies words	Identifies patterns
Factual and analytical	Conceptual and intuitive
Analyzes	Synthesizes
Detail oriented	Big picture oriented
System dominates	Imagination dominates
Has great fear of risk	Has no fear of risk
Science and math strength	Art and creativity strength
Reality based	Fantasy based
Looks at what is	Looks at what could be
Linear	Nonlinear
Orderly and methodical	Random and spontaneous

WHOLE BRAIN THINKING

Ideally, our success in almost anything, including the financial markets, requires that we become "whole brain" thinkers. Which brings us back to the idea of combining science and art as Einstein illustrates in his quote at the beginning of this book. This means we want to do our best to develop both sides of our brain and use them together to become masters of our own minds.

As nature decides, it seems that we each are born with a unique given set of attributes. Some of us are more "left brain" thinkers and some of us are more "right brain" thinkers. Then there are the lucky ones among us that are already born as "whole brain" thinkers.

NEUROPLASTICITY

They say you can't teach old dogs new tricks, which is in fact not true. It just takes a little longer to get the old dogs to create change. The brain has far greater plasticity when we are young and it gets progressively "hardwired" as we age. The good news is that recent scientific research has confirmed that the brain maintains significant plasticity even into old age. The key is to constantly work the brain, using repetition and behavior modification in order to manipulate that malleable plasticity in a way that creates your desired results.

Remember, if you don't use it, you lose it!

NEURONS AND NEURONETS

The brain is made up of approximately 100 billion tiny nerve cells called neurons. Each neuron has between 1,000 and 10,000 synapses, or places where they connect with other neurons. These neurons use the connections to form networks among themselves. These integrated or connected nerve cells form what are called neural networks or neuronets. A simple way to think about this is that every neuronet represents a thought, a memory, a skill, a piece of information, and so on.

Everyone has their own collection of experiences and skills represented in the neuronets in their brains. All those experiences shape, neurologically, the fabric of what's taking place in our perception and in our world. When we receive certain stimuli coming in from our environment, aspects of these neuronets will kick in and create chemical changes in the brain. These chemical changes in turn produce emotional reactions and condition the responses we make to the people and events in our lives.

YOU CAN REWIRE YOUR BRAIN AND YOUR TRADING

What this means is that we have the power and ability to change the neuronets in our brains if we consciously set out to do so. By using repetition and behavior modification, we can literally reprogram our brains. It is possible to rewire negative thought process into positive thought process by consciously changing our thought process. Eventually, the neuronets will rewire and the positive thought process will become "hard-wired."

KEEP AN OPEN MIND

Just keep an open mind with the information in this chapter because your mind and your brain are enormously powerful and can enable you to achieve great success.

PART IV

ART System Basics

CHAPTER 17

ART Is the Total Solution

A pplied Reality Trading—the ART system—is the total solution giving you exact entries, exits, and risk control. The system is based on the realities of the market and is designed to add structure and discipline to your trading, thus reducing stress and anxiety. ART indicates exact entries and exits based on key support and resistance levels, as well as taking into consideration market volatility.

THE FOUR ART SIGNALS

1. **The primary Pyramid Trading Point** is a trend identifier that keeps you in a trend long enough to maximize profits. Pyramid Trading Points look like triangles that indicate trend direction. Pyramid Trading Point bullish entries are confirmed once prices meet trend definitions such as higher highs (key resistance) and higher lows (key support). Bearish entries are confirmed on lower lows (key resistance) and lower highs (key support). Volatility is determined by the velocity of the left-hand side of the triangle as compared to the velocity of the right-hand side of the triangle.

2. **The minor Pyramid Trading Point** indicates only a correction in the primary trend. The primary trend is always identified by a primary Pyramid Trading Point. So the minor Pyramid Trading Point helps to identify corrections and is used as a signal to scale in or scale out of a trend. It may also be used to scalp the market.

3. **The ART One-Bar Reversal** indicates market pivot points, representing significant short-term tops and bottoms of market swings. ART Reversals are high-probability signals used for scalping, scaling out of trends, scaling in to trades, and also for countertrend trading. You can use ART Reversals in a variety of ways to compliment your trading style.

4. **The ART Two-Bar Reversal** is similar in meaning to the ART One-Bar Reversal but requires two price bars in the pattern to identify market swing pivot points.

LOADING YOUR ART SOFTWARE

Your purchase of this book entitles you to a free 30-day trial of the ART software. That way, you can see firsthand how using the ART technical analysis system can enhance your trading and investing performance.

To download your software, go to Appendix A at the back of this book or call TradersCoach.com at 1-858-695-0592.

ART SIGNALS

The variations on how and when to use these four ART signals, as shown in Table 17.1, is unlimited. Your experience and beliefs will determine how you decide to mix and match these signals to create your own custom ART system.

Your personal ART Profile (that you completed in Chapter 6 of this book) will help answer the question of what signals to use. The answer of when to use these ART signals will be based on your judgment. By studying the ART methodology, you will develop your own unique approach. Through paper-trading, your approach will be tested and you will discover what works best for you.

TABLE 17.1   ART Signals

Signal Description	Label	Icon
Primary Pyramid Trading Point	P	Triangle ▲ or ▼
Minor Pyramid Trading Point	MP	Triangle ▲ or ▼
ART One-Bar Reversal	1B	Diamond ◆
ART Two-Bar Reversal	2B	Square ■

ART COLOR MEANING

Color Meaning for Pyramid Trading Points

▲ =Yellow up-triangle: Indicates a potential bullish Pyramid Trading Point (when voided it will disappear).

▼ =Yellow down-triangle: Indicates a potential bearish Pyramid Trading Point (when voided it will disappear).

▲ =Green up-triangle: Indicates a confirmed bullish Pyramid Trading Point.

▼ =Red down-triangle: Indicates a confirmed bearish Pyramid Trading Point.

Color Meaning for ART Reversals

◆ =Green diamond: Indicates a bullish ART One-Bar Reversal.

◆ =Red diamond: Indicates a bearish ART One-Bar Reversal.

◆ =Gray diamond: Indicates a voided bullish or bearish ART One-Bar Reversal.

■ =Green square: Indicates a bullish ART Two-Bar Reversal.

■ =Red square: Indicates a bearish ART Two-Bar Reversal.

■ =Gray square: Indicates a voided bullish or bearish ART Two-Bar Reversal.

Color Meaning For ART Charts

Yellow: Indicates a potential Pyramid Trading Point.

Green: Indicates a bullish ART signal.

Red: Indicates a bearish ART signal.

Gray: Indicates a voided ART Reversal.

Black: Indicates a neutral price bar.

Note: These are the default colors for the ART Software System. You can change the defaults by referring to your *ART Trading Software User's Manual* and following the User Input instructions.

EXACT ENTRIES AND EXITS GIVE YOU STRUCTURE AND DISCIPLINE

Because ART indicates exact entries and exits that are easily seen on your chart, you know at all times whether you should be in the market or out of the market. The ART signals enable you to avoid random trades and help eliminate emotional trading. You want to avoid emotional trading since it leads to poor trading.

The ART signals allow you to trade confidently. This lowers your stress and anxiety, which allows you to remain calm by making rational, objective, and sound trading decisions. We call this *adding structure to your trading.*

By adding structure to your trading, you can overcome psychological barriers that may be keeping you from attaining trading success. For example, traders experiencing fear and emotional discomfort while trading usually lack structure and/or confidence in their trading. ART not only deals with these issues but enables you to reach higher levels of trading mastery.

Few will argue that, today more than ever before, traders and investors have an overwhelming amount of information available to absorb, analyze, and process. Too much market information can cause you unnecessary stress and it can impair your abilities. By the time you absorb and process this excessive information, you may miss some fantastic trades! By keeping signals easily visible on your chart depicting exact entries and exits, ART eliminates this information analysis paralysis.

CHAPTER 18

Pyramid Trading Points (P and MP)

A significant change in the market, represented by price action, is defined as a Pyramid Trading Point, which looks like a triangular Egyptian pyramid, hence the name. ART Reversal bars are commonly found at the apexes (pointed peaks) of Pyramid Trading Points. Please make note of the following abbreviations, which are used throughout the text:

- P = Primary Pyramid Trading Point
- MP = Minor Pyramid Trading Point
- PTP = Pyramid Trading Point

MINOR PYRAMID TRADING POINTS

The Minor Pyramid Trading Points can be used to:

1. Identify market corrections and consolidations in primary trends.
2. Scale out of trends.
3. Countertrend trade.
4. Scalp trade.

Sometimes, the primary Pyramid Trading Point occurs at market fractals and at key reversal points. When you look at a chart, you can easily see the primary Pyramid Trading Point. It forms during tops and bottoms of market thrusts and pullbacks, which represent price highs and lows. The

ART charting software identifies all Pyramid Trading Points as colored triangles that look like pyramids on your chart.

Potential Pyramid Trading Point: When prices have not yet exceeded the point, or apex, of the triangle will appear yellow in software.

Confirmed Pyramid Trading Point: When prices exceed the point, or apex, of the triangle will appear red or green in software.

PYRAMID TRADING POINT RULES

The rules for entries and exits based on a Pyramid Trading Point signal are illustrated in Figure 18.1 and Figure 18.2.

Figure 18.3 illustrates Bullish (triangles facing upward) and Bearish (triangles facing downwards) Pyramid Trading Points. Figure 18.3 also shows that prices must retrace enough to form a triangle of some degree.

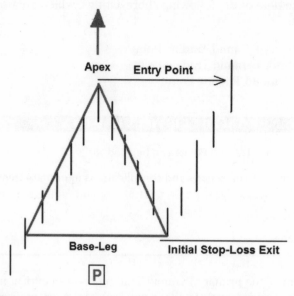

FIGURE 18.1 Bullish Pyramid Trading Point Trading Rules: Apex always points in the direction of the trend; Enter one-tick above the Apex; Initial Stop-Loss Exit one-tick below the Base-Leg

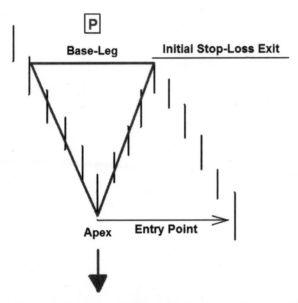

FIGURE 18.2 Bearish Pyramid Trading Point Trading Rules: Apex always points in the direction of the trend; Enter one-tick below the Apex; Initial Stop-Loss Exit one-tick above the Base-Leg

MOMENTUM AND NEW INFORMATION

When a Pyramid Trading Point forms on your chart, momentum has changed, which causes the Pyramid Trading Point. Maybe a news-related item came out or momentum in the existing trend dried up.

The next thing to realize about the Pyramid Trading Point is that if prices exceed a pivot whether to the upside or downside, some new information came into the market for traders to feel differently. Maybe momentum returns or the "smart money" knows something we don't.

Whatever the reason, all we know is that the market is pushing prices beyond the old behavior that stopped it before. This alone may be a reason to enter a trade. Your reasons for trade entry will be further strengthened with high volume.

PYRAMID TRADING POINT REQUIREMENTS

The minimum requirements of a bullish Pyramid Trading Point are two previous bars with higher highs and higher lows and the following two bars of lower highs and lower lows. The minimum requirements of a bearish

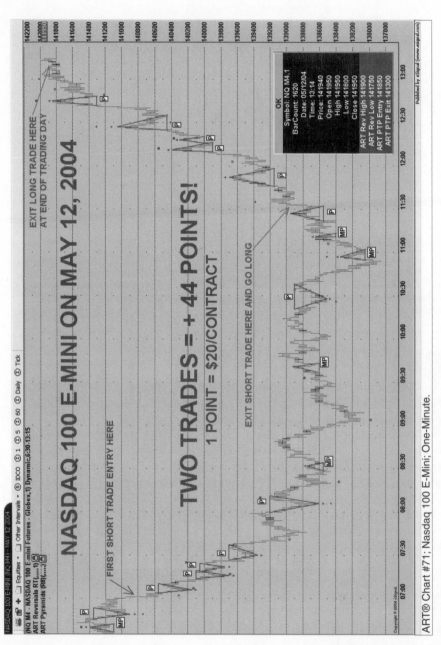

FIGURE 18.3 Bullish and Bearish Pyramid Trading Points
Source: eSignal. www.eSignal.com

Pyramid Trading Point are two previous bars with lower highs and lower lows and the following two bars of higher highs and higher lows.

When prices pull back more than the minimum requirements, you can draw the base leg of the Pyramid Trading Point.

The ART trading software takes into consideration minimum Pyramid Trading Point requirements along with other momentum characteristics when identifying a Pyramid Trading Point. The ART software looks for the highest-probability Pyramid Trading Point and may pass on some even though they meet the minimum requirements.

In most cases, the ART charting software will draw a yellow-colored Pyramid Trading Point before the signal is confirmed so that you know its strength and have time to calculate your correct trade size.

 COLOR MEANING FOR ART CHARTS

- Yellow pyramid: Potential (bullish or bearish) Pyramid Trading Point. This indicates a potential trade is developing. This will give you time to prepare for the trade and calculate your trade size.
- Green pyramid: Confirmed bullish Pyramid Trading Point.
- Red pyramid: Confirmed bearish Pyramid Trading Point.

THE PYRAMID TRADING POINT PROVIDES YOU WITH VALUABLE MARKET INFORMATION

The Pyramid Trading Point gives you a variety of valuable market information:

1. Trend direction
2. Trend-trade entry points
3. Trend-trade exit points
4. Trend exhaustion
5. Market truths
6. How to identify trend corrections using minor Pyramid Trading Points
7. How to trade from a "bracketed market"

1. TREND DIRECTION

The Pyramid Trading Point looks like a triangle when drawn on a chart. The apex of the triangle always points in the direction of the trend (either bullish or bearish). Using the Pyramid Trading Point makes trend trading easier. It is hard to miss the trend if you know how to properly use the Pyramid Trading Point.

Figure 18.4 shows you how the Pyramid Trading Point triangles point in the direction of the trend. The bearish Pyramid Trading Point points downward in the direction of the downtrend, and the bullish Pyramid Trading Point points upward in the direction of the uptrend.

2. TREND-TRADE ENTRY POINTS

When drawn, a Pyramid Trading Point becomes confirmed only when prices exceed the apex of the Pyramid Trading Point triggering the trade entry. Until the apex is exceeded, the Pyramid Trading Point is considered to be a potential Pyramid Trading Point and will remain yellow in color.

When the apex of a primary Pyramid Trading Point is exceeded, it signals a trend is in place. An entry signal is triggered when prices exceed the apex by one or two ticks. The logic behind this signal is that some new information came into the market, causing prices to end their correction. This establishes the base leg of a Pyramid Trading Point. When prices move past the apex of the Pyramid Trading Point, this triggers your signal.

With a bullish Pyramid Trading Point, positive information came into the market, causing prices to go higher and exceed the apex. With a bearish Pyramid Trading Point, negative information came into the market, causing prices to go lower and below the apex. You do not care what the information is, because you know price action is a real truth and that is what triggers the ART signals.

3. TREND-TRADE EXIT POINTS

Most trading systems use a moving average to exit trades. Moving averages are usually derivatives of price and do not represent the truth of the market. Furthermore, moving averages can be adjusted with variables such as simple versus compounded.

Using the Pyramid Trading Point, you are trading with market truths. You will set your stop-loss exit at the base leg of the pyramid. A trade exit signal is generated when prices reverse one tick past the base leg.

If prices reverse and pass the Pyramid Trading Point base leg, then some new information came into the market, causing the reversal. We exit the trade based on price activity, which is a truth of the market.

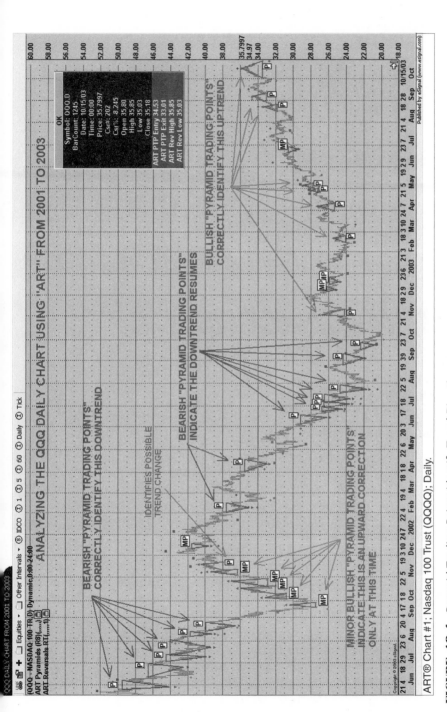

FIGURE 18.4 Pyramid Trading Points Identify Trend Direction

Source: eSignal. www.eSignal.com

4. TREND EXHAUSTION

Counting the number of consecutive Pyramid Trading Points can help determine when a trend is nearing exhaustion. We have determined that four or five consecutive primary Pyramid Trading Points in the same direction indicates a mature trend nearing its end.

5. MARKET TRUTHS

The Pyramid Trading Point represents market truths and displays the current behavior of traders in the market. Using the Pyramid Trading Point allows you to trade the realities of the market without distorting the market. The Pyramid Trading Point tells you when to enter a trade based on price activity as it is currently happening.

6. HOW TO IDENTIFY TREND CORRECTIONS USING THE MINOR PYRAMID TRADING POINT

Using the rules and definitions of a minor Pyramid Trading Point, we can quickly distinguish between the dominant trend and a minor trend correction.

Minor Pyramid Trading Point

A minor Pyramid Trading Point is often the first Pyramid Trading Point that forms in the opposite direction of the primary trend. A minor Pyramid Trading Point occurs when prices have still not exceeded the base leg of the most recent Pyramid Trading Point of the primary trend.

When prices exceed the base leg of the most recent dominant trend Pyramid Trading Point, then the next Pyramid Trading Point that occurs in the direction of the existing minor Pyramid Trading Point will be considered a primary Pyramid Trading Point.

Figure 18.5 illustrates the concept of the minor Pyramid Trading Point identifying a trend correction.

The two bullish Pyramid Trading Points in Figure 18.5 are minor bullish Pyramid Trading Points because the prices at the apex of these Pyramid Trading Points are below the base leg of the most recent bearish Pyramid Trading Point. When prices get above that base leg, then all bullish Pyramid Trading Points will be primary Pyramid Trading Points, indicating a change in trend to the upside.

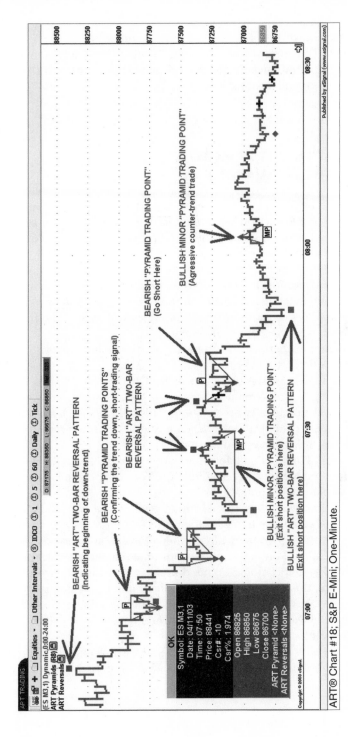

FIGURE 18.5 Minor Pyramid Trading Points (MP) Identify Trend Corrections

Source: eSignal. www.eSignal.com

Figure 18.6 illustrates a change in trend without any minor Pyramid Trading Point. The first bullish Pyramid Trading Point is not a minor Pyramid Trading Point because the apex is above the base leg of the most recent bearish Pyramid Trading Point.

 7. HOW TO TRADE FROM A "BRACKETED MARKET"

At times a market will remain "bracketed" for a certain period of time. Usually, significant trends occur when a market breaks the channel or bracket. This can be a great trading opportunity. The Pyramid Trading Point can help you catch these significant trends emerging from bracketed markets. (See Chapter 26 for more information on bracketed markets.)

Figure 18.7 illustrates how to use the Pyramid Trading Point to catch trends from a bracketed market. The Pyramid Trading Point apex is a trade entry. When markets break their brackets, prices will exceed the Pyramid Trading Point and trigger your trade entry.

This five-minute chart is an example of price consolidation for the S&P e-mini (ES H4) contract on February 4, 2004.

The consolidation on this chart is from 8:00 AM (PST) to 10:10 AM (PST). The yellow triangles, green diamonds, and red squares are signals from the Applied Reality Trading software program. The yellow triangles are called *potential* Pyramid Trading Points. When a number of them form next to each other, they indicate a consolidation.

The Pyramid Trading Point apex indicates where you would enter your trade at the outer edges of this consolidation. Your initial stop loss or trade exit would be placed just outside the base leg.

Figure 18.8 shows when prices broke outside the consolidation on February 5, 2004 (compare this with Figure 18.7).

The market breaks dramatically to the downside and the bearish yellow Pyramid Trading Points turn red, confirming the new downtrend. The bullish yellow Pyramid Trading Points disappear because they were never confirmed. Here, the consolidation went longer and became narrower. In addition, a new aggressive bearish Pyramid Trading Point formed in the narrowest part of the consolidation and would have put you short at the best possible point.

Figure 18.9 is an example of how the ART charting software identifies market consolidations and brackets the market in preparation for a new trade.

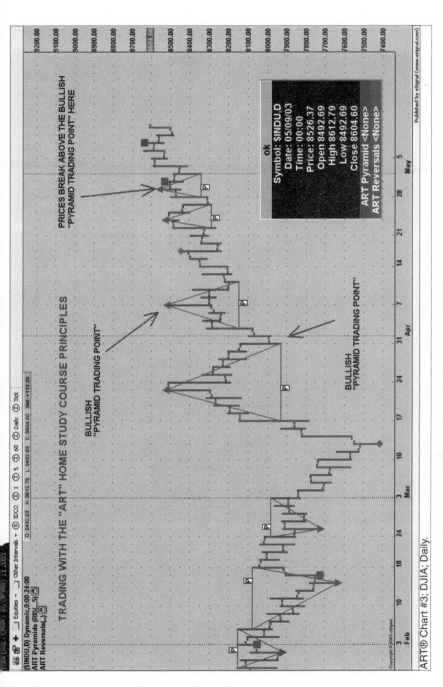

ART® Chart #3; DJIA; Daily.

FIGURE 18.6 Quick Trend Correction Occurs with No Minor Pyramid Trading Point
Source: eSignal. www.eSignal.com

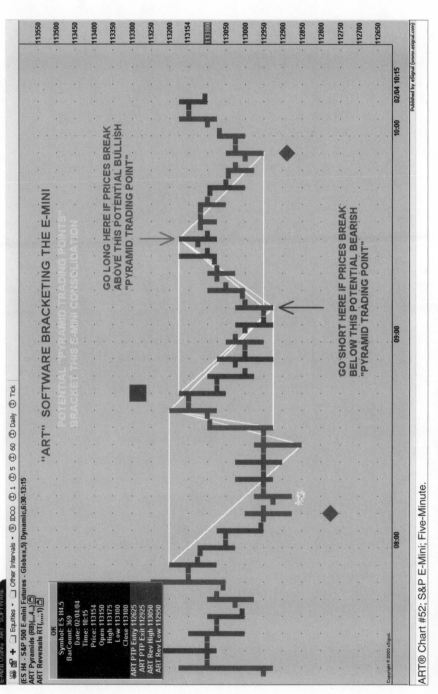

FIGURE 18.7 Classic Bracketed Market with Pyramid Trading Point Pattern

Source: eSignal. www.eSignal.com

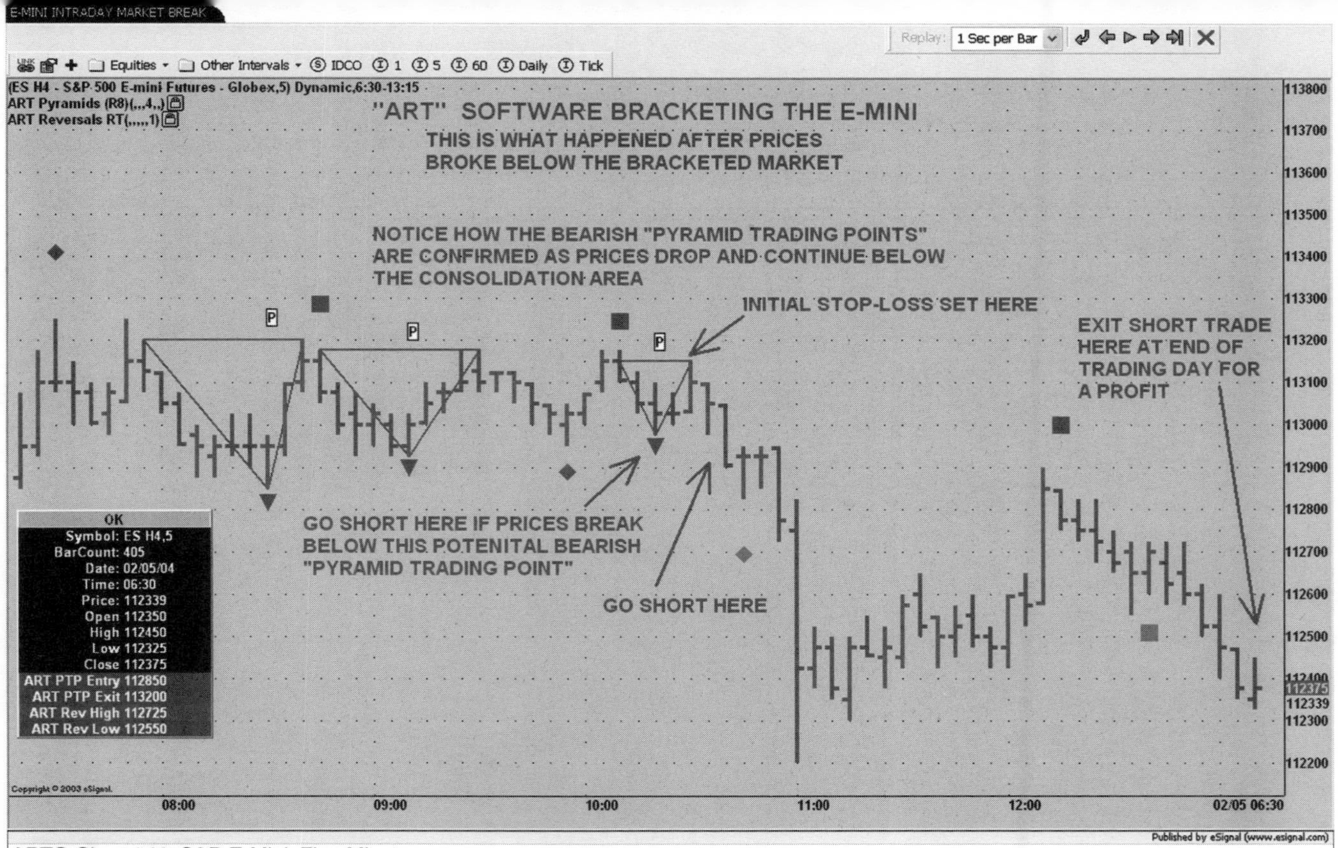

EMINI INTRADAY MARKET BREAK

FIGURE 18.8 Bracketed Market from Figure 18.7 Breaks to the Down Side
Source: eSignal. www.eSignal.com

109

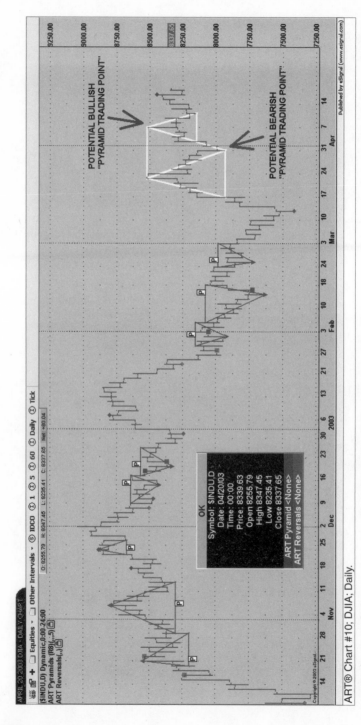

FIGURE 18.9 Multiple Pyramid Trading Points in this Pattern Indicate a Bracketed Market

Source: eSignal. www.eSignal.com

ART® Chart #10; DJIA; Daily.

The ART charting software identifies the consolidation by bracketing it with bullish yellow and bearish yellow Pyramid Trading Points. When prices break out, regardless of direction, the Pyramid Trading Point that gets confirmed will trigger a trade.

CUSTOMIZING THE ART SOFTWARE TO TAILOR IT TO YOUR NEEDS

The ART trading software has many features that can be adjusted to suit your needs and to suit changing market conditions such as market volatility. You will want to refer to the *User's Manual* that you download from the www.TradersCoach.com web site to give you the step-by-step instructions on how to change the default settings that are set up in the software when you first receive it. Two of the most popular features are MinScore and Audio Technology.

ADJUSTING THE MINSCORE FOR A PYRAMID TRADING POINT

MinScore—Default value is 5. This is used to calculate the score of the conditions that make up the "peaks and valleys" used to identify the Pyramid Trading Point patterns.

This is a numeric input with a range of values from 1 to 8. This input controls how well formed the pyramids must be before they are selected as a Pyramid Trading Point.

Increasing the MinScore value will cause the ART Pyramid Trading Point system to identify only the higher-scoring peaks and valleys. Lowering this value will cause the ART Pyramid Trading Point system to identify lesser-scoring peaks and valleys.

Setting this to 1 will result in Pyramid Trading Points being identified that are less constrictive in nature, while a setting above 5 will be more constrictive.

Under perfect conditions, the highs and lows of these bars would ascend smoothly up and down, as shown in Figure 18.10.

The pyramids in Figure 18.11 would get scores of 7, 6, and 5, respectively, because the shape of the pyramid gets progressively more ragged as the highs and lows fall out of line.

The MinScore input controls the minimum score and therefore how well formed a Pyramid Trading Point must be before it is selected by the software.

"Perfect Pyramid"

FIGURE 18.10   Perfect Pyramid with a MinScore of 8. NOTE: This diagram is for illustrative purposes only

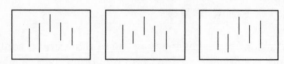

FIGURE 18.11   Less Perfect Pyramids with a MinScore of "7," "6," and "5," Respectively. NOTE: These diagrams are for illustrative purposes only

MinScore value of 1 is very tolerant, and it will allow many small pyramids. A value of about 4, 5, or 6 seems to work best. Values of 7 and 8 are very selective. This leads to some fairly large pyramids with a higher probability.

ADJUSTING THE AUDIO TECHNOLOGY FOR YOUR PYRAMID TRADING POINT

One of the most popular features of the ART trading software is that you can set specific voices and tones to signal to you that there is a "Pyramid Trading Point Entry Now" or a "Pyramid Trading Point Exit Now." You will actually hear either a tone or a man's voice or a woman's voice that tells you when to enter and exit a trade. Or you can set the software to a variety of tones such as a door opening or a door closing.

The value of this feature is that you can multitask yet avoid missing important entries and exits, and you don't need to constantly keep your eyes on the computer screen. This will reduce fatigue and stress for you.

IDENTIFYING TREND EXHAUSTION

The Pyramid Trading Point can be used to gauge when a trend may exhaust itself. Most trends end after four consecutive Pyramid Trading Points in the same direction.

Usually, all trends end after five consecutive Pyramid Trading Points in the same direction.

At times, significant trends may have eight or more consecutive Pyramid Trading Points in the same direction before the trend changes. The most significant trends occur when traders on other time frames are participating in the trend as well.

GETTING AGGRESSIVE

After four consecutive Pyramid Trading Points, you can get aggressive in trading corrections. This may enable you to catch the next trend in the opposite direction.

For example, you could trade ART Reversals going against the trend and all minor Pyramid Trading Points going against the trend. You should wait until you get four consecutive Pyramid Trading Points pointed in the same direction, and trade with the trend. After four consecutive Pyramid Trading Points, then you can become more aggressive and look for quality countertrend trades.

Extended trends can have far more consecutive Pyramid Trading Points than just four. Don't consider a countertrend trade until you have had at least four consecutive Pyramid Trading Points. After you gain experience in the market you are trading, you may conclude that four Pyramid Trading Points is not the right number for you—maybe it should be five or six, for example.

Check the higher-time-frame charts for trend verification to gauge the strength of the trend you are currently analyzing. This will help you determine trend exhaustion. If the trend on the higher time frame is mature and nearing exhaustion, that is a confirmation signal that the trend is nearing an end.

Likewise, if there is no apparent trend on the higher time frame, that is indicating the trend you are experiencing on your time frame may not be significant. Look for it to end in four or five Pyramid Trading Points. If there is an apparent trend on the higher time frames, and the trend is just beginning, you may get more than five consecutive Pyramid Trading Points on your lower time frame.

Test and paper-trade to determine the optimal number of Pyramid Trading Points that signal trend exhaustion for you. Practice using higher time frames to help determine if the trend is significant. Once you have determined that a trend is near exhaustion, you may want to use ART Reversals or minor Pyramid Trading Points to enter new aggressive countertrend trades.

This may enable you to catch the new emerging trend early.

PYRAMID TRADING POINT SUMMARY

Understanding how to use the Pyramid Trading Point will be an important tool for you in your trading. By now, you should understand how to use Pyramid Trading Points not only to enter the market but also to quickly identify the trend.

The ART charting software is flexible in that you can adjust the strictness of the Pyramid Trading Point using MinScore. You have been provided with the rules that allow flexibility in your trading. But you also have structure in defining a qualified Pyramid Trading Point.

CHAPTER 19

Market Truths: Price Bars and Volume

I n this chapter, you will learn that ART has a different definition of a bullish and bearish price bar than most systems do. And, you'll see how volume can have great meaning depending on its intensity. These two truths combined give you the ultimate undistorted reality of the markets.

THE FIRST MARKET TRUTH IS PRICE

ART uses a simple Open, High, Low, Close price bar. A price bar tells us a lot about what is going on between buyers and sellers. The current price bar tells us what the reality is *now*—not tomorrow, not yesterday, nor one minute ago.

Price bars tell us not only the price of the market you are looking at but also more about who is in control in the market. An individual price bar can also indicate the possibility of a reversal in the trend. We can compare the current price bar with the previous one, which tells us how the market is doing now compared to one price bar ago.

New information coming into the market will cause traders to either buy or sell. This will cause the price to change. The outcome of that action is represented in the price bar. By comparing the current price bar to the previous price bar, we can see that this new information had either a positive effect or a negative effect on price.

Either way, you are looking at how the market is responding to new information such as a news event. In the ART approach to price bar meaning, it is important to realize that ART determines if a price bar is bullish or bearish by where prices *close* in relation to where prices have traveled on the price bar itself. Notice I did not say *open*.

 COLOR MEANING FOR ART PRICE BARS

1. Bullish price bar = Green
2. Neutral price bar = Black
3. Bearish price bar = Red

Note: These are the default colors. You can change the defaults by referring to your *ART Software User's Manual* and following the "User Input" instructions.

ART DEFINES PRICE BARS DIFFERENTLY

1. ART defines a *bullish price bar* as one where prices close on the upper half of the price bar.
2. ART defines a *bearish price bar* as one where prices close on the lower half of the price bar.

ART PRICE BAR POSSIBILITIES

Given that the definition of an ART price bar is different than other systems' definitions, here are a few possibilities you should be aware of:

- It is possible to have a bearish price bar (by the ART definition) even though prices go higher than the previous price bar's close.
- It is possible to have a bearish price bar (by the ART definition) when the close is higher than the open on the same price bar.
- It is possible to have a bullish price bar (by the ART definition) even though prices go lower than the previous price bar's close.
- It is possible to have a bullish price bar (by the ART definition) when the close is lower than the open on the same price bar.

Remember: With ART a bullish or bearish price bar is determined based on where the *close* is in relation to the price bar interval (the distance between the price bar's high and low price). If the open and close are both exactly at the 50 percent mark on the price bar, then the bar is "neutral," with little meaning except that the bulls and bears are in stalemate.

By evaluating the market's response to new information (by concentrating on the close) instead of evaluating the new information itself, you are tuned in to the reality of the marketplace. Don't look at the content of any news event because the content is more information than you need.

SEVEN ART PRICE BAR DEFINITIONS

How a price bar opens and closes is an important truth we must be aware of. Here are examples of ART price bar definitions:

1. **Bullish: Closing price at the very top of the price bar.** Means buyers are in control.

2. **Bullish: Closing price on the top half of the price bar.** Means buyers are in control. Not as bullish as if price is on the very top of the bar (the higher prices are on the price bar, the more bullish the bar is).

3. **Bearish: Closing price on the very low of the price bar.** Means sellers are in control.

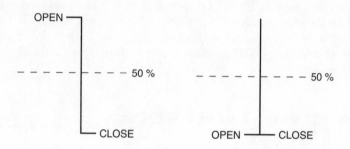

4. **Bearish: Closing price on the lower half of the price bar.** Means sellers are in control. Not as bearish as if price is on the very low of the price bar (the lower the prices are on the bar, the more that sellers are in control).

5. **Bullish: Closing price is above the opening price of the price bar (and is exactly at the 50% mark on the price bar).** Means buyers are in control.

6. **Bearish: Closing price is below the open of the price bar (and is at exactly the 50% mark on the price bar).** Means sellers are in control.

```
                              |
                              |
           OPEN ——|
           — — — —|—— CLOSE — — 50 %
                              |
                              |
```

7. **Neutral: Closing price is equal to the opening price (and is at exactly the 50 percent mark on the price bar).** Means buyers and sellers are in stalemate.

```
                        |
                        |
     — —OPEN ——|—— CLOSE — — - 50 %
                        |
                        |
```

ELONGATED PRICE BAR

A large price range has significant meaning and is called an *elongated price bar*. This type of price bar is at least one third longer than the previous three to five price bars. Elongated price bars can signal the beginning or end of a trend. Since the ART software identifies all ART Reversals, it does not need to identify elongated ART Reversals. When you see an ART One-Bar Reversal that is elongated, it represents high emotions in the market between buyers and sellers and is one of the highest probability ART One-Bar Reversal signals.

THE SECOND MARKET TRUTH IS VOLUME

Volume is a market truth because it represents the number of trades (activity) in the current price bar. Like price, volume is not distorted; it is actual activity, a truth. Using volume along with price allows us to see what the market is saying. It is a powerful combination. Most indicators are derived from either volume or price. The problem is that indicators can be "tweaked." And guess who does the tweaking? That's right, humans!

When a trader tries to tweak the variables of an indicator, the truth can be distorted. You may ask, then, why do they do it? The answer is that they are looking for the "Holy Grail"—the magic indicator that will solve all their trading problems and make trading a sure thing. The other reason is that the media has brainwashed traders into believing they must have these indicators to be successful.

One positive note about indicators is that once you realize mentally that they are not the truth of the market and that they can cause destructive opinions, they can be useful. (This is an advanced technique; see Part V of this book). These indicators are useful only if you are mentally tough enough to resist forming destructive opinions. Use indicators only as a confirmation tool. ART does not use indicators to forecast the market.

THE MEANING OF VOLUME

The meaning of volume is determined by its intensity. Here are two ways volume can have meaning:

1. *Volume is higher than the previous price bar.* More traders are trading. It may be bullish or bearish, depending on how the price is moving. The more volume a price bar has, the more significant it is. The more volume present, the less likely it is to have price manipulation from locals on the floor or market makers. An increase in volume usually means trades are coming in from outside the community of locals and market makers. This means that new information has entered the market causing traders to increase volume.

2. *Volume is higher as compared to the last 20 price bars.* This has great significance and means many traders are trading. New information has come in, causing traders to trade with increased activity. Prices have reached an emotional point and traders are either panicking out of the market or are trying to get into the market. It can also be a combination of fear and greed. The two groups of buyers and sellers cause high volume. This type of activity usually occurs around market tops or market bottoms. It can also occur during breakouts when buyers want to buy the market.

CHAPTER 20

ART Reversal Bar Signals (1B and 2B)

N ow, we're going to work on combining price bar information with volume information. By combining these two market truths, we can benefit from significant signals called *ART Reversal bar signals*. ART reversals can be used in a variety of ways that you will learn about in this chapter. Please make note of the following abbreviations that are used throughout the text:

- 1B = ART One-Bar Reversal
- 2B = ART Two-Bar Reversal

ART REVERSALS

Both the ART One-Bar Reversal and Two-Bar Reversal can be used for:

1. Scaling out of trends
2. Scaling in to trends
3. Scalping
4. Countertrend trading
5. Getting an early signal of change in trend

The ART One-Bar Reversal occurs at market tops and bottoms. It is often seen as an elongated price bar at the end of a runaway market trend. This is a strong trading signal with relatively low risk. You will know, within five bars after entering the trade, if this trade is going to be successful or not.

The ART charting software identifies all ART Reversal bars (both One-Bar and Two-Bar Patterns) and is designed to be flexible enough to accommodate your style of trading. This flexibility allows you to set the ART Reversals to occur aggressively or conservatively. (See the *ART Charting Software User's Manual* that you downloaded from the www. TradersCoach.com web site to learn how to optimize this software to your needs.)

ON-SCREEN ICONS FOR ART REVERSALS

♦ = Green diamond: Bullish ART One-Bar Reversal

♦ = Red diamond: Bearish ART One-Bar Reversal

♦ = Gray diamond: Voided bullish or bearish ART One-Bar Reversal

■ = Green square: Bullish ART Two-Bar Reversal

■ = Red square: Bearish ART Two-Bar Reversal

■ = Gray square: Voided bullish or bearish ART Two-Bar Reversal

Note: These are the default colors. You can change the defaults by referring to your *ART Trading Software User's Manual* and following the "User Input" instructions.

HIGHEST-PROBABILITY ART ONE-BAR REVERSAL

1. **Elongated price bar.** At least one third longer than the previous five bars. Some reversals do occur on nonelongated price bars as long as the volume is high and the trend has been sharply in place. When you see an ART One-Bar Reversal that is elongated, it represents high emotions in the market between buyers and sellers. It is the highest-probability ART One-Bar Reversal signal.

2. **Increasingly high volume.** As compared to previous price bars volume. Better yet, higher volume than the previous two price bars.

Once you see an elongated price bar with increasingly high volume, you have a high-probability ART One-Bar Reversal. Not all ART One-Bar Reversals are elongated, but when you see one that is, it is a high-probability trade.

The ART One-Bar Reversal signal becomes void if prices go one tick beyond the opposite side of the reversal bar before triggering our expected trade. If this happens, it indicates a possible trade in the other direction.

Also, a new ART One-Bar Reversal cancels the previous ART Reversal price bar signal. As long as prices stay inside the highs and lows of the reversal bar, the signal(s) remain valid.

What we will not know when trading this technique is if the reversal will be a major change in trend or just a normal correction in the ongoing trend. You must accept this. Your personality will determine if and how you trade this technique.

ART 1B RULES

Bullish ART 1B Rules

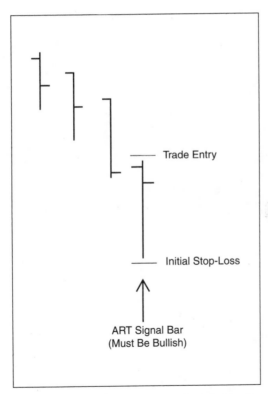

- The signal price bar is identified by a green icon below the signal price bar on the chart.
- Go long on the next bar if prices go one tick above this ART One-Bar Reversal signal price bar.

- Set your initial stop loss one tick below the bullish ART One-Bar Reversal signal price bar.

- Signal is voided if prices on the next bars go below the ART One-Bar Reversal signal bar before going above it.

Bearish ART 1B Rules

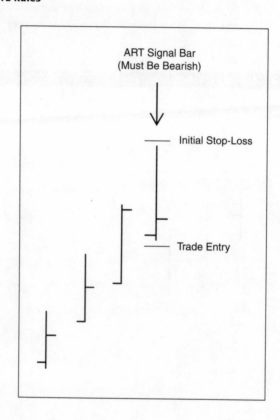

- The ART One-Bar Reversal signal price bar is identified by a red icon above the signal price bar on the chart.

- Go short on the next bar if prices go one-tick below this ART One-Bar Reversal signal price bar.

- Set your initial stop loss one tick above the high of the bearish ART One-Bar Reversal signal price bar.

- Signal is voided if prices on the next bars go above the ART One-Bar Reversal signal bar before going below it.

THREE METHODS OF MONITORING AN ART ONE-BAR REVERSAL TRADE

1. *Trading as a possible beginning of a new trend in the opposite direction.* Keep your stop in place until you have your first correction in the new trend. Once this new trend resumes and forms a new high, move your initial stop loss up one tick under the first pullback. Keep doing this until you either get stopped out or you see a sharp increase in the current trend. Then look for a reversal bar to get out, or get out and do a stop and reverse.

   Figure 20.1 illustrates many examples of ART One- and Two-Bar Reversal signals on increasing volume along with adjusted stops.

2. *Trading as if this is a correction in the current trend and not a change in trend direction.* Once you initiate a trade against the trend, keep your initial stop loss in place. Then look for an ART Reversal, indicating that the correction is possibly over. If you are trading this as a correction, the best you should expect from the trade is that the correction will retrace the trend by 50 percent. The idea is to take a quick profit.

   Figure 20.2 shows a bearish trend trade on an intraday chart with an exit at the end of the trading day. However, there is also a countertrend trade opportunity: the pullback in the downtrend-trend as indicated by the bullish ART One-Bar Reversal occurring at approximately 12:30 PM on this one-minute S&P e-mini chart.

   This countertrend trade off that bullish ART One-Bar Reversal would have been at an approximate price of $1130.50. As prices rebound, you would not know if the downtrend would continue or not, but the primary bearish Pyramid Trading Point indicates that the trend is still down. However, this rebound or countertrend movement of prices provides an excellent opportunity to countertrend trade using the bullish ART One-Bar Reversal. You could exit this countertrend trade when prices retrace 50 percent of the downtrend or wait until the next bearish ART signal, indicating a possible resumption of the downtrend.

3. *Trading as if this is a new trend in the opposite direction, but getting out if it appears to be just a correction in the current trend.* Once you initiate a trade against the trend, keep your initial stop loss in place. When prices move 50 percent against the trend, use a trailing stop on half your positions. If your stop is triggered, you then are long half your original size. Keep the stop for your remaining position at the original stop-loss location. Either you now will get stopped out or a new trend will emerge. Then you can revert to placing stops in accordance with the trend.

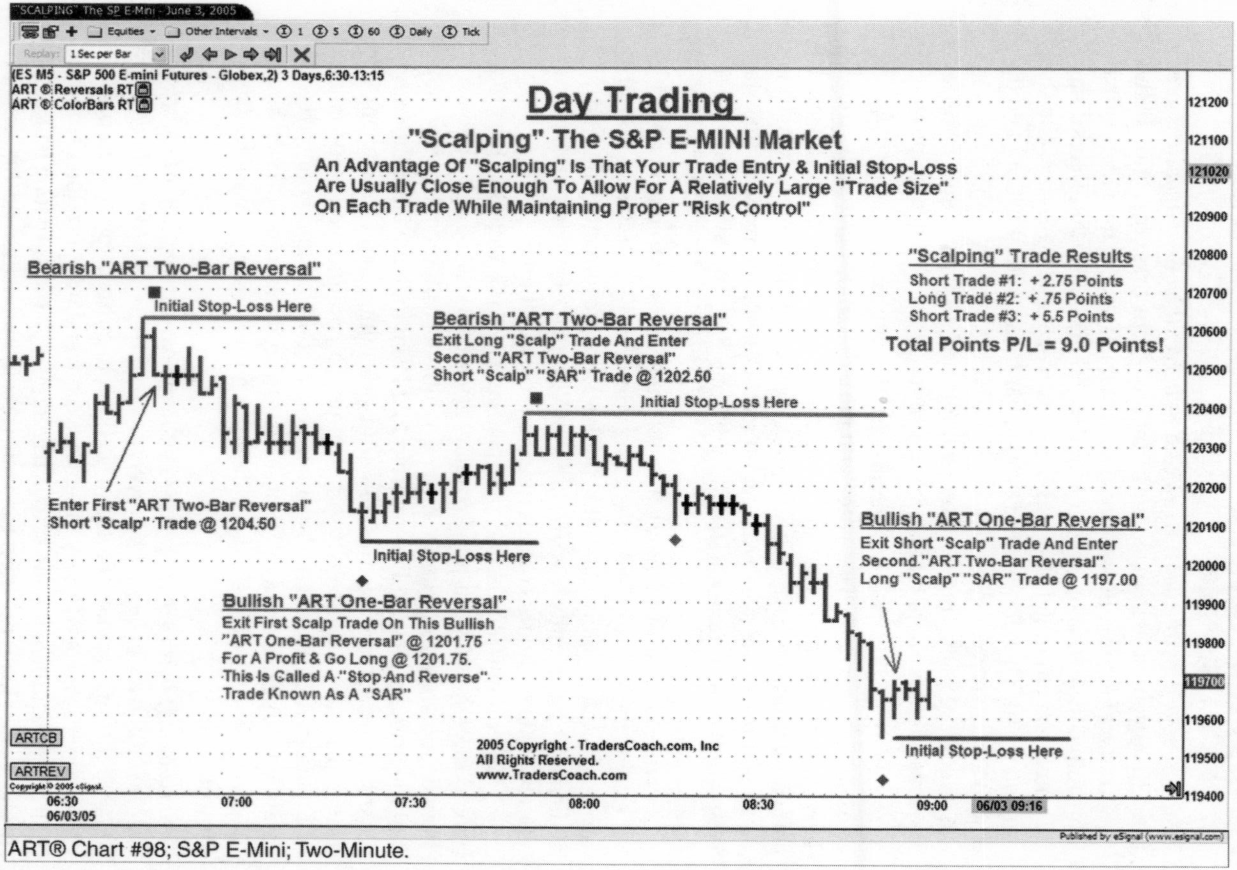
"SCALPING" The SP E-Mini - June 3, 2005
(ES M5 - S&P 500 E-mini Futures - Globex,2) 3 Days,6:30-13:15
ART ® Reversals RT
ART ® ColorBars RT
Day Trading
"Scalping" The S&P E-MINI Market
An Advantage Of "Scalping" Is That Your Trade Entry & Initial Stop-Loss
Are Usually Close Enough To Allow For A Relatively Large "Trade Size"
On Each Trade While Maintaining Proper "Risk Control"
Bearish "ART Two-Bar Reversal"
Initial Stop-Loss Here
Enter First "ART Two-Bar Reversal"
Short "Scalp" Trade @ 1204.50
Bearish "ART Two-Bar Reversal"
Exit Long "Scalp" Trade And Enter
Second "ART Two-Bar Reversal"
Short "Scalp" "SAR" Trade @ 1202.50
Initial Stop-Loss Here
Initial Stop-Loss Here
Bullish "ART One-Bar Reversal"
Exit First Scalp Trade On This Bullish
"ART One-Bar Reversal" @ 1201.75
For A Profit & Go Long @ 1201.75.
This Is Called A "Stop And Reverse"
Trade Known As A "SAR"
"Scalping" Trade Results
Short Trade #1: + 2.75 Points
Long Trade #2: + .75 Points
Short Trade #3: + 5.5 Points
Total Points P/L = 9.0 Points!
Bullish "ART One-Bar Reversal"
Exit Short "Scalp" Trade And Enter
Second "ART Two-Bar Reversal"
Long "Scalp" "SAR" Trade @ 1197.00
Initial Stop-Loss Here
2005 Copyright - TradersCoach.com, Inc
All Rights Reserved.
www.TradersCoach.com
ARTCB
ARTREV
06:30
06/03/05
07:00
07:30
08:00
08:30
09:00
06/03 09:16
121200
121100
121020
120900
120800
120700
120600
120500
120400
120300
120200
120100
120000
119900
119800
119700
119600
119500
119400
Published by eSignal (www.esignal.com)
ART® Chart #98; S&P E-Mini; Two-Minute.

FIGURE 20.1 ART One- and Two-Bar Reversals Are Shown with Square and Diamond Icons
Source: eSignal. www.eSignal.com

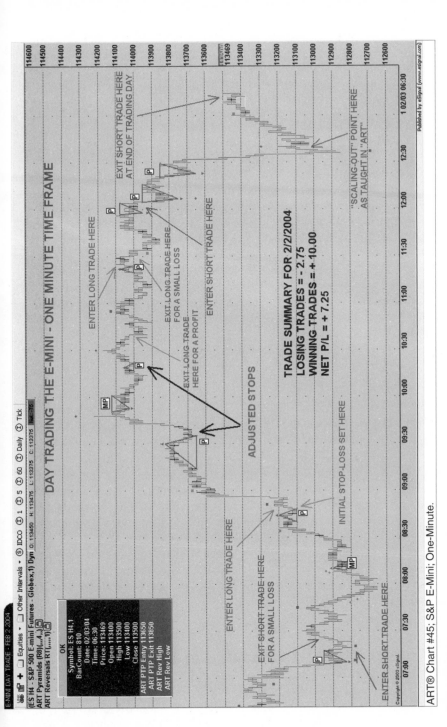

ART® Chart #45; S&P E-Mini; One-Minute.

FIGURE 20.2 Countertrend Opportunity

Source: eSignal. www.eSignal.com

Figure 20.3 illustrates a change in trend using the ART charting software. Note the elongated bullish ART Reversal bar at the bottom of the trend.

UNEXPECTED TRADES IN THE OPPOSITE DIRECTION

If an ART One-Bar Reversal forms but the market moves in the opposite direction of the expected trade, this can be a powerful signal.

For example, either a bullish or bearish trade could be taken from the same ART One-Bar Reversal signal price bar. To do this, you would bracket the ART One-Bar Reversal signal price bar by one tick, and when the market goes above the signal price bar, you buy the market; when prices go below the signal price bar, you sell ("short") the market.

Another way to use this strategy is if we already have a position in the market. If an ART One-Bar Reversal forms but the market does not reverse off this bar and instead continues to trend, then we could use this to add on to our position size.

So this ART One-Bar Reversal could be used:

1. As a stop to exit a trend trade.
2. To add on to a trend trade.
3. As a stop and reverse (SAR) if we are aggressive and want to reverse our position in hopes to catch a trend in the opposite direction early.

Figure 20.4 illustrates the two gray-colored bearish ART One-Bar Reversals occurring in November when prices are moving sharply upward. These gray-colored bearish diamonds indicate ART One-Bar Reversals that were voided out because the market was bullish. However, if you missed the Pyramid Trading Point trend trade entry in October, then you could have entered your bullish trade when prices voided out either one of these bearish ART One-Bar Reversals, which means you could have entered your bullish trade as prices went above the highs of each of those signal bars indicated by the gray diamonds.

USING THE INSIDE PRICE BAR TO GET AN EARLY ENTRY

This technique is used to get into a reversal trade sooner than waiting for the standard entry on the ART One-Bar Reversal. This signal gets you into

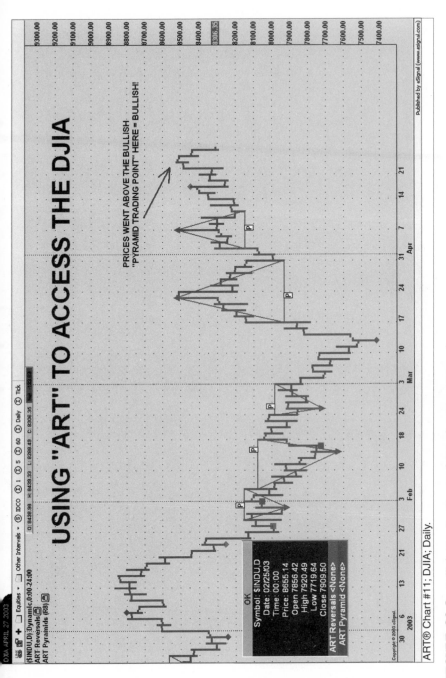

FIGURE 20.3 Bullish One-Bar Reversal Signals a New Uptrend
Source: eSignal. www.eSignal.com

129

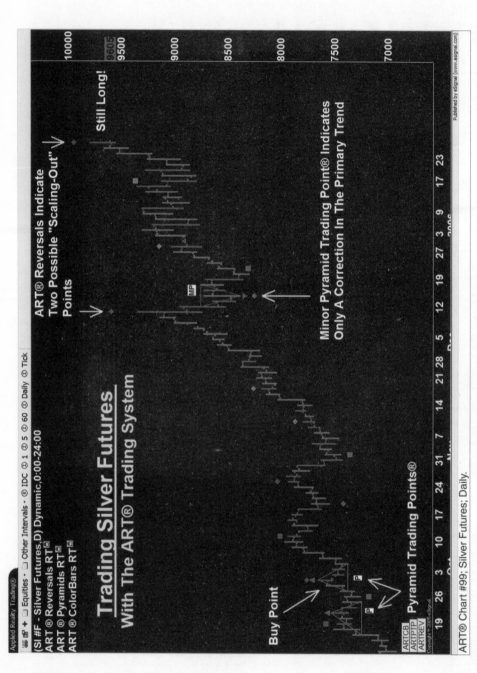

FIGURE 20.4 Voided Bearish ART One-Bar Reversals Are Bullish Entry Signals

the market with a closer stop loss, which allows for a larger trade size compared to the standard ART Reversal bar entry.

The ART charting software labels the ART One-Bar Reversal with a diamond. Then the market has to form an inside bar, a price bar located after the ART Reversal signal bar that has a high and low that is inside the signal bar's high and low price. If an inside bar forms, move your trade entry from the ART Reversal signal price bar to the high or low of the inside bar, depending on if we are going long or short (the ART charting software does not label this inside bar trade).

The signal generated by the inside bar is only in the direction of the anticipated or expected reversal trade originally generated by the ART One-Bar Reversal.

The initial stop loss for a bullish trade can either be one tick under the original ART Reversal bar or one tick under the inside bar. Use the ART Reversal bar as your initial stop loss.

ART TWO-BAR REVERSAL

We talked about the ART One-Bar Reversal. Now we are going to cover the ART Two-Bar Reversal pattern, which means the trade setup is based on two price bars, and is identified by the ART charting software.

Figure 20.5 illustrates the elongated bullish ART Reversal bar formed on May 23 that begins the new bullish trend. This is an example of using an ART Reversal to enter a new emerging trend after the rules of trend exhaustion have been met. Pyramid Trading Points soon emerge, and then several other ART Reversals forms at key pivot points, indicating short-term swings in this market. Some of these bearish ART Reversals can be used to scale out of the trend with part of your position or scalp out of the trend with your entire position if you are a scalper, while some of the bullish ART Reversals can be used to scale in to the trend known as *adding on* to your current trend position. Note that bullish ART Reversals can also be used to set trailing stops if you desire. The stop-loss placement would be under the low of the most recent bullish ART Reversal in the uptrend. This can be helpful in markets where prices have moved far away from the current Pyramid Trading Point base leg stop-loss level.

ART REVERSALS TELL YOU WHEN THE TREND ENDS

If trends don't end on an ART One-Bar Reversal bar, then they will usually end on an ART Two-Bar Reversal pattern. So, one way or another, we are

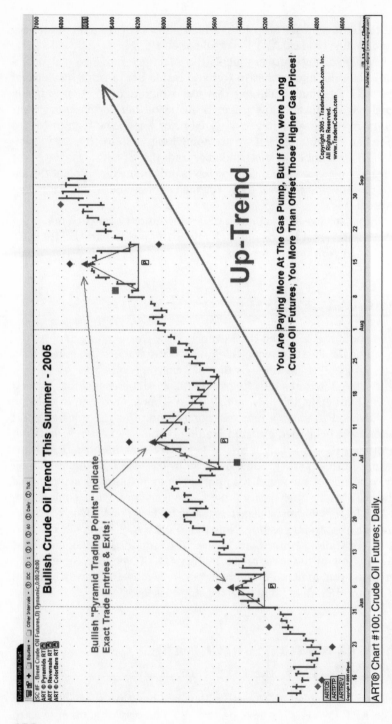

FIGURE 20.5 Elongated Bullish ART One-Bar Reversal Forms on May 23
Source: eSignal. www.eSignal.com

going to have a high probability of spotting a potential change in trend from the ART Reversal signals.

Because we are using two bars instead of one (with the ART Two-Bar Reversal), volume may not be as high as the volume on other bars. This is why no volume minimums are required on this setup. If high volume is present, the ART Two-Bar Reversal patterns will have a significantly higher probability of success.

When intraday trading below the five-minute time frame, the ART Two-Bar Reversal pattern is more common than the ART One-Bar Reversal.

In fast time frames like a one-minute chart, new information coming into the market may take two price bars to represent itself. The ART Two-Bar Reversal catches this phenomenon.

 ART 2B RULES

Bullish ART 2B Rules

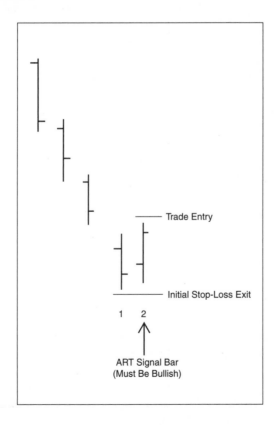

- The bullish ART Two-Bar Reversal signal bar is identified by a green icon below it.
- Go long on the next price bar if prices go one tick above the signal bar.
- Set your initial stop loss one tick under the low of the first price bar in the bullish ART Two-Bar Reversal pattern.
- Signal is voided if prices on the next price bars go below the signal bar before going above it.

Bearish ART 2B Rules

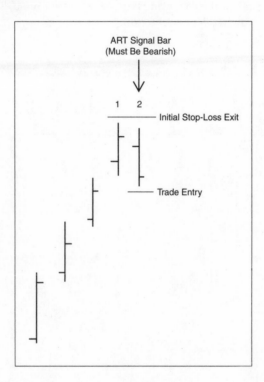

- The bearish ART Two-Bar Reversal signal bar is identified by a red icon above it.
- Go short on the next price bar if prices go one tick below the signal bar.
- Set your initial stop loss one tick above the high of the first price bar in the bearish ART Two-Bar Reversal pattern
- Signal is voided if prices on the next price bars go above the signal bar before going below it.

CHAPTER 21

Trend-Trading Rules

I f you are a trend trader, you are looking for markets where prices are moving significantly in a certain direction, either up or down. Trend traders try to find trending markets early enough to profit before the trend ends.

Investors, position traders, and even day traders can all be trend traders. There are many types of trends, from intraday trends lasting several minutes to long-term trends lasting days, weeks, months, and even years. In this book, you have learned about how the ART system identifies trends using the Pyramid Trading Point trend indicator and how you can implement techniques that will help maximize your profit from trends.

10 ART RULES FOR TREND TRADING

Follow these rules for your trend trading and investing. Look at Figure 21.1 to see trend-trading with the ART system. See Figures 21.2 and 21.3 for illustrations of these rules.

1. Trade the first (primary) P labeled Pyramid Trading Point in a new primary trend. Enter one tick beyond the apex and set your initial stop loss one tick beyond the base leg.

2. Calculate your trade size to risk no more than 2 percent of your trading account.

135

"TREND TRADING" WITH "ART"

GO LONG HERE

EXIT LONG TRADE HERE
FOR A PROFIT

GO SHORT HERE

INITIAL SHORT TRADE STOP-LOSS

TRAILING STOPS

PROFITABLE TRADE AND STILL SHORT!

ART® Chart #70; LSI Logic Corp; Daily.

FIGURE 21.1 Trend Trading with ART

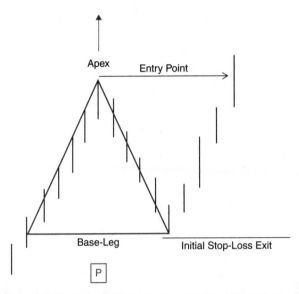

FIGURE 21.2 Bullish Pyramid Trading Point Trading Rules: Apex always points in the direction of the trend; Enter one-tick above the Apex; Initial Stop-Loss Exit one-tick below the Base-Leg

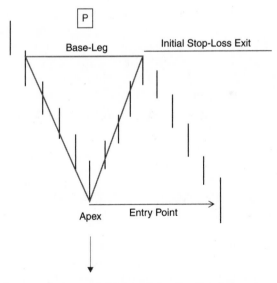

FIGURE 21.3 Bearish Pyramid Trading Point Trading Rules: Apex always points in the direction of the trend; Enter one tick below the Apex; Initial Stop-Loss Exit one tick above the Base-Leg

3. If the market moves in your favor and your initial position is profitable enough, then you can decide to scale out of 33 percent of your positions so you at least break even if the initial stop loss is hit on your remaining positions. Always wait for an ART signal to scale out.

4. If your initial stop loss is never hit, then adjust your stops (trailing stops) as new primary Pyramid Trading Points occur.

5. If a trend develops and you get four consecutive primary Pyramid Trading Points in the same direction (an indication of trend exhaustion), you can scale out of positions using the ART Reversals in the opposite direction of the trend you are in.

6. After four consecutive Pyramid Trading Points, you may want to be aggressive and trade the next minor Pyramid Trading Point in the opposite direction. Caution: Some powerful trends will have more than four consecutive primary Pyramid Trading Points.

7. Consider any minor MP labeled "Pyramid Trading Point" as a countertrend trade or as a scaling-out opportunity.

8. All minor Pyramid Trading Points labeled "MP" and ART Reversal bar patterns with entries that are not in the direction of the primary trend are considered countertrend trades and should be used for scaling out of trend trades only.

9. If you want to scale in to trades or add on to your current position, use additional "P" labeled "Pyramid Trading Points" and/or "ART Reversals" with entries in the direction of the trend. Do this only when your trade is profitable (when your stop loss would generate a profit if you were stopped out), and when your money management allows. ART Reversal bar patterns on extremely high volume are significant.

10. Eventually, you will be stopped out, preferably at a profit. Always adhere to your stop exit.

REMEMBER, THE TREND IS YOUR FRIEND; FEAR IS YOUR ENEMY!

Trend traders are usually on the correct side of significant market moves. Big trends are what make trend traders profitable. Missing these trends makes trend traders unprofitable. Significant trends usually occur after periods of volatility. This causes the unprofitable traders to second-guess themselves because of the fear of being stuck in volatility again and incurring more losses.

Missing the next big trend is disastrous!

Fear is generated by a variety of factors personal to each trader. If you feel fear, you must ask yourself why. Your answer will determine your weakness as a trader. Deny your weaknesses and your losses will create more fear, which will again remind you of your weaknesses—hence the snowball effect.

When this occurs enough, you will either work to overcome your weaknesses, quit trading, or go bust. You will choose the path of least resistance.

A trader's improperly managed fear can manifest losing trades even with a well-tested and sound trading system or approach.

CHAPTER 22

Countertrend-Trading Rules

I f you are a countertrend trader, you are looking for markets where there is a correction in the overall trend. The concept behind countertrend trading is to find trending markets that are either overextending and ready to correct or are in the beginning of a correction.

Countertrend traders make a profit taking trades against the trend. This is risky because you are going against the flow of the trending market, and while many traders can do well with this technique, you will need to develop your skills. Once corrections end, prices can quickly rebound back in the direction of the trend. You will need to stay alert when countertrend trading.

Investors, position traders, and even day traders can all be countertrend traders. ART Reversals and minor Pyramid Trading Points are used to identify countertrend trades with the ART system.

FIVE ART RULES FOR COUNTERTREND TRADING

Follow these rules for your countertrend trading and investing. Look at Figure 22.1 to see countertrend-trading with the ART system.

1. Primary P labeled Pyramid Trading Point indicates trend direction.
2. All Minor MP labeled Pyramid Trading Point and ART Reversal patterns with entries that are not in the direction of the primary trend are considered entry signals for countertrend trades.

141

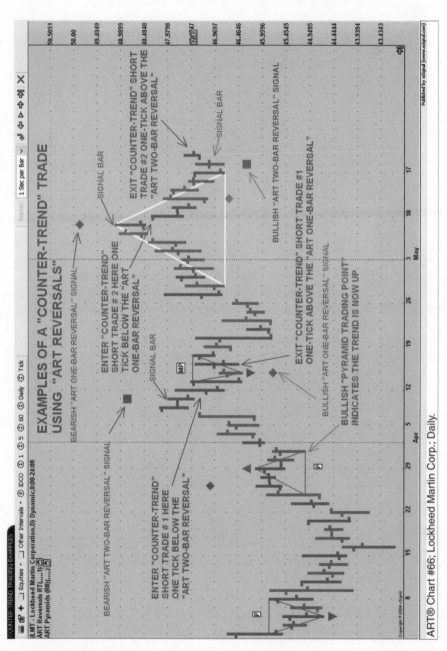

FIGURE 22.1 Countertrend Trading with ART

Source: eSignal. www.eSignal.com

3. The best countertrend trade entries occur after four consecutive primary P labeled Pyramid Trading Points have been confirmed. The probabilities of catching a new significant trend in the opposite direction are high.

4. Close your position when prices retrace 38 percent to 50 percent of the primary trend or when your trailing stop loss is triggered.

5. ART Reversals on extremely high volume are significant. ART Reversals occurring on elongated price bars are significant.

There are many ways you can use the ART signals to countertrend trade. You can use just the ART Reversals that form against the primary trend as identified by the Primary Pyramid Trading Point. Or you can use just a minor Pyramid Trading Point for your entry against the primary trend and then exit on the next bullish ART Reversal or wait until another minor Pyramid Trading Point to trail your countertrend trade stop loss. Experiment and test to see which combinations work best on the markets you like to trade.

 1B COUNTERTREND RULES

Bullish ART 1B Countertrend Rules:

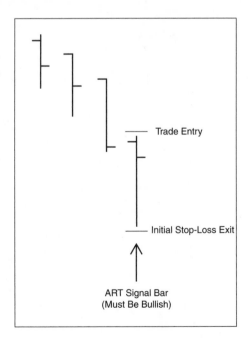

- The signal price bar is identified by a green diamond icon below the signal price bar on the chart.
- Go long on the next bar if prices go one tick above this ART One-Bar Reversal signal price bar.
- Set your initial stop loss one tick below the bullish ART One-Bar Reversal signal price bar.
- Signal is voided if prices on the next bars go below the ART One-Bar Reversal signal bar before going above it.

Bearish ART 1B Countertrend Rules

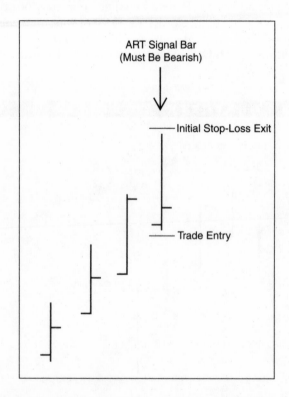

- The ART One-Bar Reversal signal price bar is identified by a red diamond icon above the signal price bar on the chart.
- Go short on the next bar if prices go one tick below this ART One-Bar Reversal signal price bar.

- Set your initial stop loss one tick above the high of the bearish ART One-Bar Reversal signal price bar.
- Signal is voided if prices on the next bars go above the ART One-Bar Reversal signal bar before going below it.

 2B COUNTERTREND RULES

Bullish ART 2B Countertrend Rules

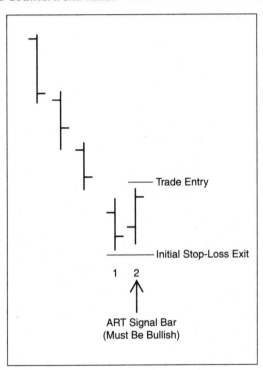

- The Bullish ART Two-Bar Reversal signal bar is identified by a green square icon below it.
- Go long on the next price bar if prices go one tick above the signal bar.
- Set your initial stop loss one tick under the low of the first price bar in the Bullish ART Two-Bar Reversal pattern.
- Signal is voided if prices on the next price bars go below the signal bar before going above it.

Bearish ART 2B Countertrend Rules

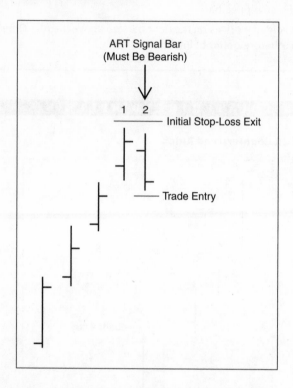

- The Bearish ART Two-Bar Reversal signal bar is identified by a red square icon above it.
- Go short on the next price bar if prices go one tick below the signal bar.
- Set your initial stop loss one tick above the high of the first price bar in the bearish ART Two-Bar Reversal pattern.
- Signal is voided if prices on the next price bars go above the signal bar before going below it.

CHAPTER 23

Scalping Rules

I f you are a scalp trader, you are looking to take quick profits from the market. You look for opportunities in short-term price swings in various market conditions such as in bracketed or channeling markets where prices swing between the high of the bracket or channel and the low of the bracket or channel. Scalpers trade between bullish and bearish or bearish and bullish ART Reversals in these various market cycles. There are many variations of scalping.

Scalping is different from countertrend trading in that scalping does not always take place in a trend environment, whereas countertrend trading does. A countertrend trade is always entered on the corrections of a trend. When you are a scalper yes you can scalp corrections, but you can also scalp in a bracketed sideways market where no trend is in place. When you are scalping there is also the tendency to have a faster paced program than if you are countertrend trading.

SCALPING VARIATIONS

1. Scalping in a consolidated market between ART Reversals with SARs: Trading between the ART Reversals using stop and reverse (SAR) orders (always being in the market and not caring about trend direction, scalping in the direction of the trend, or scalping against the trend).

2. Scalping in the direction of the trend: Using ART Reversal entry in the direction of the trend as defined by the most recent Pyramid Trading Point.

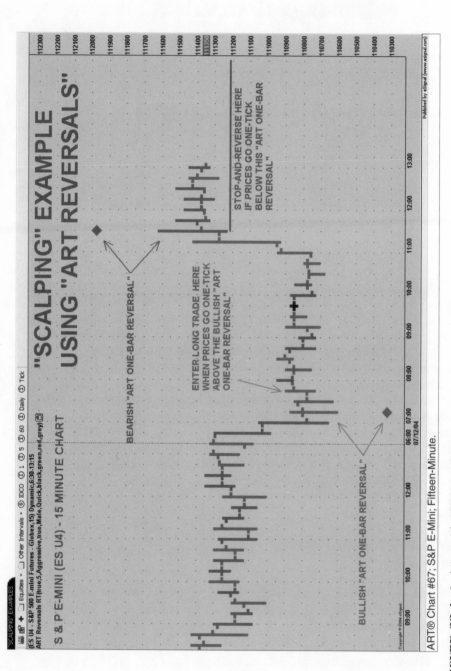

FIGURE 23.1 Scalping with ART Using SARs
Source: eSignal. www.eSignal.com

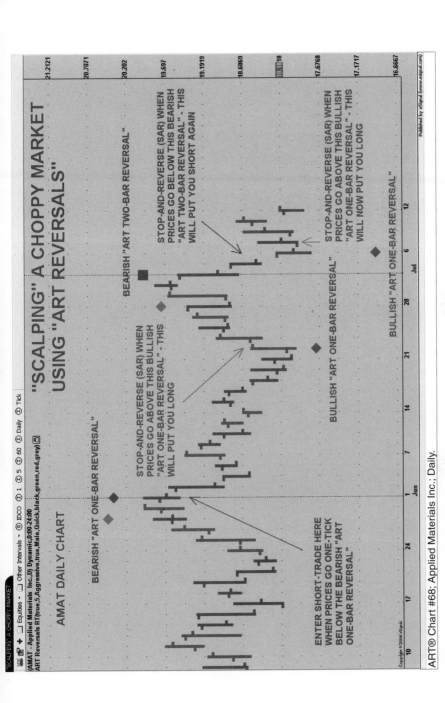

FIGURE 23.2 Scalping with ART in a Choppy Market
Source: eSignal. www.eSignal.com

149

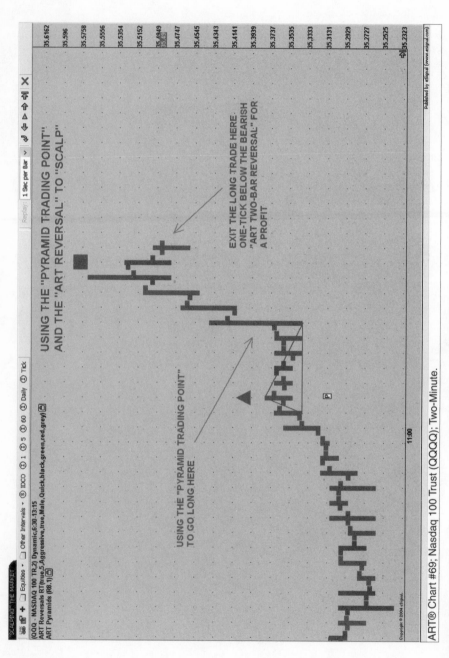

FIGURE 23.3 Using the Pyramid Trading Point and ART Reversals Together for Scalp Trades

Source: eSignal. www.eSignal.com

3. Scalping against the direction of the trend: Using ART Reversal entry in the opposite direction of the trend as defined by the most recent Pyramid Trading Point (countertrend scalp).

4. Scalping in the direction of the trend with a PTP entry and a Reversal bar exit: Pyramid Trading Point entry and then next exit on the next ART Reversal in the opposite direction.

ART Reversals on extremely high volume are significant. ART Reversals occurring on elongated price bars are significant.

Figure 23.1 illustrates how to integrate ART Reversals and SARs when scalping.

ART Reversals can be used to scalp quick profits from choppy markets, as illustrated in Figure 23.2.

Figure 23.3 illustrates how to integrate the Pyramid Trading Point and the ART Reversals when scalping.

 1B SCALPING RULES

Bullish ART 1B Scalping Rules

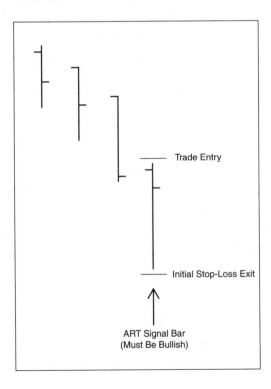

Trade Entry

Initial Stop-Loss Exit

ART Signal Bar
(Must Be Bullish)

- The signal price bar is identified by a green diamond icon below the signal price bar on the chart.

- Go long on the next bar if prices go one tick above this ART One-Bar Reversal signal price bar.

- Set your initial stop loss one tick below the bullish ART One-Bar Reversal signal price bar.

- Signal is voided if prices on the next bars go below the ART One-Bar Reversal signal bar before going above it.

Bearish ART 1B Scalping Rules

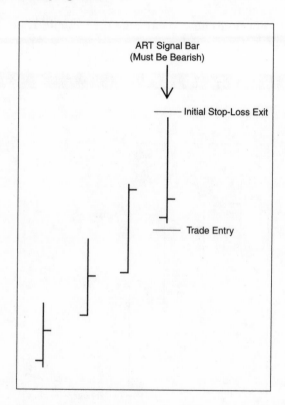

- The ART One-Bar Reversal signal price bar is identified by a red diamond icon above the signal price bar on the chart.

- Go short on the next bar if prices go one tick below this ART One-Bar Reversal signal price bar.

- Set your initial stop loss one tick above the high of the bearish ART One-Bar Reversal signal price bar.
- Signal is voided if prices on the next bars go above the ART One-Bar Reversal signal bar before going below it.

 2B SCALPING RULES

Bullish ART 2B Scalping Rules

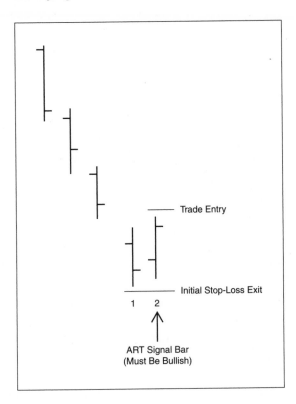

- The Bullish ART Two-Bar Reversal signal bar is identified by a green square icon below it.
- Go long on the next price bar if prices go one tick above the signal bar.
- Set your initial stop loss one tick under the low of the first price bar in the bullish ART Two-Bar Reversal pattern.
- Signal is voided if prices on the next price bars go below the signal bar before going above it.

Bearish ART 2B Scalping Rules

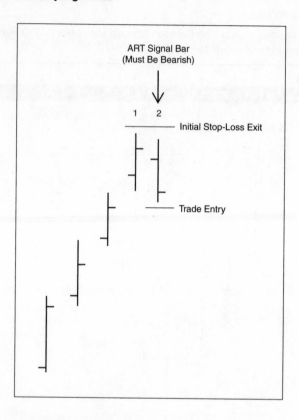

- The bearish ART Two-Bar Reversal signal bar is identified by a red square icon above it.
- Go short on the next price bar if prices go one tick below the signal bar.
- Set your initial stop loss one tick above the high of the first price bar in the bearish ART Two-Bar Reversal pattern.
- Signal is voided if prices on the next price bars go above the signal bar before going below it.

PART V

Advanced Techniques

CHAPTER 24

When to Use Advanced Techniques

T his ART Advanced Techniques section will show you how to apply master techniques to your trading and utilize the ART trading software to its fullest potential. It is recommended that you use them after you have become experienced trading the ART system.

TWO DEFINITIONS

1. *Grounded assessments:* Trading and investing rules, techniques, and approaches that trade the markets as they unfold. (*Example:* Trade entries and exits based purely on price and volume.)

2. *Ungrounded assessments:* Trading and investing rules, techniques, and approaches that trade the markets by trying to forecast the markets. (*Examples:* MACD, stochastics, Elliott Wave, and anything that involves a forecast.)

ART focuses primarily on trading the markets using only grounded assessments. Combining ungrounded assessments with the ART grounded assessments trading rules is an advanced technique and is not recommended for all traders.

You must fully realize and understand how ungrounded assessments can cause you to form opinions regarding market direction, and this can lead to poor trading. Use ungrounded assessments not as "holy grails," but as "tools" in your trading arsenal.

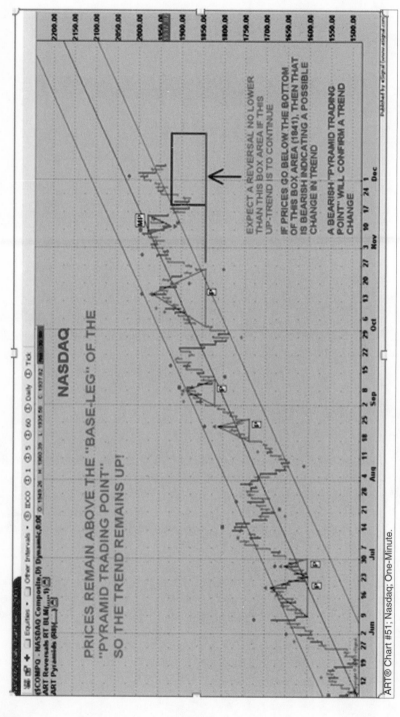

FIGURE 24.1 Bullish Trend Channel with ART

Source: eSignal. www.eSignal.com

Experienced traders know how to handle multiple trading tools, and they don't fall prey to forecasting illusions. Ungrounded assessments can at times benefit or round out their overall trading.

WHEN TRADING ART WITH UNGROUNDED ASSESSMENTS, FOLLOW GUIDELINES A AND B

A. If the forecasted trend direction is not in alignment with the trend as identified by using the ART trading software you have two options:

1. Pass on the trade.
2. Trade in the direction of the trend as defined by the ART approach, but use aggressive ART trade stop-loss exits.

B. If the forecasted trend direction is in alignment with the trend as identified by the ART trading software, you can be more liberal with your trade stop-loss exits. ART is your primary approach at all times and overrides any ungrounded assessment forecast.

The advanced techniques in this section can enhance your trading performance. Paper-trade these ideas to determine the best way to use them.

USING TREND CHANNELS

Trend channels are also useful tools. Here is how they work:

- ART Reversal bar trading at the extreme outside edges of the trend channel.
- Confirmation of a trend.
- Stops either below or above the outer channel in breakaway markets.

Figure 24.1 illustrates a bullish trend channel. ART Reversal bar long trades could have been taken in the direction of the trend when prices corrected to the bottom of the lower edge of the trend channel.

CHAPTER 25

Scaling Out and Scaling In

S caling out of positions is one of my favorite advanced techniques since it locks in profit and reduces stress. The goal of trend trading is to stay in the trend as long as possible. Sometimes when a trend takes off and skyrockets into a profitable zone, it is very difficult to resist the temptation to liquidate and take all of your profit. Scaling out enables you to get the best of both worlds. You can take some of your position off the table and lock in profit and then let the rest of your trade continue until you get stopped out.

SCALING OUT OF POSITIONS

Scaling out of trades is a technique that can convert some losing trades into profitable ones, reduce stress, and increase your bottom line. You can use scaling-out techniques for trend trading, scalping, and ART Reversal bar trading. And it works on *all* time frames.

It is important to reduce stress while you're in a trade. Then you can focus on the trade and not be subject to emotions such as fear and greed. Properly scaling out of positions can make you not only more profitable, but it can also significantly reduce stress.

In order to scale out of trades your initial trade size must be large enough so you can reap the benefits of scaling out. The technique is applicable for both long and short positions, and for all markets including futures, stocks, indexes, and options. Your initial position or trade size should always be within a 2 percent risk parameter. The key is to initiate a large enough trade size while not risking more than 2 percent on entering the trade.

KEEP RISK WITHIN 2 PERCENT

For our purposes we will assume that your money management trading rules require that you risk no more than 2 percent on any one trade. Given that rule we need to be careful when increasing trade size to use the scaling out technique.

There are two ways to increase your trade size and keep risk within 2 percent:

1. Find a market that you can initiate a large enough trade size with your current trading account based on a 2 percent or less loss if this initial position is stopped out.
2. Add additional trading capital to your trading account to allow for a larger position. Two percent of a larger account allows for a larger trade size.

Another alternative is to use the leverage of options, but you must be familiar with options, their "time value" decay, delta, etc. Using options would be considered a specialty or advanced technique, and if you are not familiar with them, this method could lead to increasing your stress and your potential risk.

SCALING OUT EXAMPLE

Using the e-mini as an example, your account size is $25,000 and you choose to risk 2 percent on this trade. Two percent of $25,000 is $500. Your trade entry is 1037.75 and your exit is 1036.25 so you can buy approximately six contracts and stay within your risk parameters.

If you get stopped out before having a chance to scale out, your loss would only be 2 percent, which is acceptable from a risk-of-ruin standpoint. Therefore, this potential risk should not create any stress.

When your trade becomes profitable scaling out comes into play. There are many variations to this technique, so you will need to paper-trade to find what works best for you. You may want to enter trades using the

Pyramid Trading Point and scaling out of your position when an ART Reversal bar forms in the opposite direction of your trade.

As soon as the trade is profitable enough, cover part of your position and liquidate enough contracts so that if you are still stopped out at your initial stop loss, you will still make a profit. If the trade becomes even more profitable and you still have a large enough trade size, then you may want to liquidate more contracts to lock in additional profit.

If your initial stop loss is never triggered, then you should be able enjoy the rest of the trade and let it go as long as the trend continues, knowing that no matter what happens at the very least you will make a profit on this trade.

If you trade only one or two contracts you really can't scale out of positions in a meaningful way. This is another reason why larger trading accounts have an advantage over smaller ones. Also, some markets are more expensive than others, so the cost of the trade will determine your trade size. Remember in choosing your market, liquidity is important, and you must have sufficient market liquidity to execute scaling out of positions.

Note: Poor fills due to poor liquidity can adversely affect this scaling-out technique.

The psychology of scaling out is to reduce stress by locking in profit, which should help you stay in trends longer with your remaining positions.

Figure 25.1 and Figure 25.2 illustrate scaling out on an intraday time frame.

The initial trade size was calculated using the 2 Percent per Trade Risk Rule, based on the trade entry and the initial stop-loss point as indicated on the chart.

Scaling out can be used in all markets and on all time frames. Stops are adjusted and positions are scaled out in increments as part of this money management program.

SCALING IN TO POSITIONS

Scaling in is used when you are in a trend, and you want to be aggressive and get as large a position as possible as the trend moves in your favor. You must scale in to a trade only when it is profitable because you never want to risk more than 2 percent on any one trade. When scaling in, you will be adding to your position when additional ART entry signals are triggered while you are already in a profitable trade.

You cannot use scaling out of positions at the exact same time as when you are scaling in to positions because these two techniques are in direct conflict. You can however scale in and scale out during the period of one

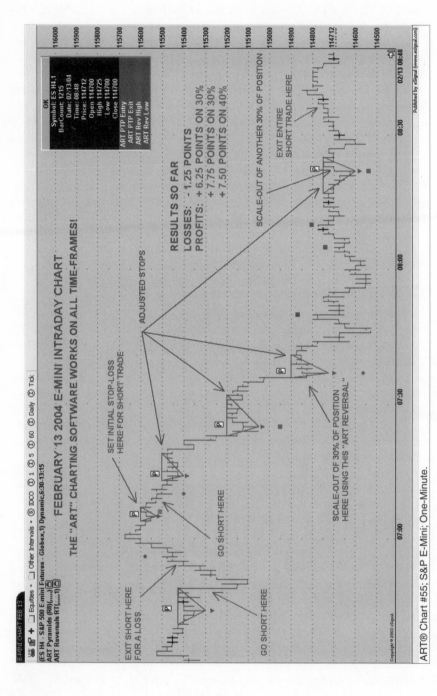

FIGURE 25.1 Scaling Out 30 Percent of Your Position to Lock in Profit and Relieve Anxiety

ART® Chart #55; S&P E-Mini; One-Minute.

164

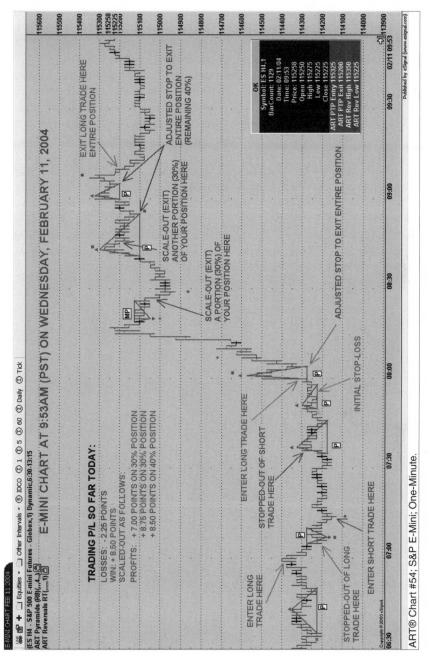

FIGURE 25.2 Scaling Out 30 Percent of Your Position to Lock in Profit and Relieve Anxiety

Source: eSignal. www.eSignal.com

trend trade. Each technique has its benefits and traders may at times switch between scaling out and scaling in depending on the trade or market they are trading. Also your psychology will determine which technique is best for you.

There are many variations but the key is to remember to use scaling in only when you are already profitable; never add on to a losing position. You may *not* want to scale in once four consecutive Pyramid Trading Points have been confirmed in the same direction. The reason for this is that after four Pyramid Trading Points, the probabilities of a trend correction or change in trend is high. You may not want to be scaling in at this point in a trend that is due for correction.

Note: At times some significant trends can have eight or more Pyramid Trading Points before the trend changes!

As stated earlier, usually significant trends occur when traders on other time frames are participating in the trend as well. If this is the case, you have a higher chance of getting more Pyramid Trading Points on the time frame you are trading. The trend may be one that lasts longer because of so many traders participating in the trend, causing it to extend.

CHAPTER 26

How to Trade Bracketed Markets

T here are several ways to trade bracketed markets, and your style will dictate your approach. Trend traders, scalpers, and option traders will use bracketed markets differently because their style will require different techniques. In this chapter, we will explore a variety of techniques to apply to bracketed markets.

WHAT'S ANOTHER NAME FOR A BRACKETED MARKET?

There are many names for a bracketed market, and this can be confusing to the new trader or investor. We wanted to list the variety of names that all have the same meaning as a bracketed market. Throughout this book, we will try to refer to this type of market with one name, and that is *bracketed*. But, on occasion in this book, and in other books you are likely to see the following AKA (also known as) terms:

- Consolidated
- Channeled
- Sideways
- Nontrending
- Range-bound
- Choppy
- Sleepy
- Drunk

For the record, the definition of a *bracketed market* is: A market that is stuck in a price range between an identifiable "resistance" and "support" level. On a chart, a bracket will be seen as a sideways horizontal line. Some of the most powerful and profitable trends come out of markets that have been bracketed for more than 20 price bars. You will want to scan markets to find ones that are bracketing so that you can place a trade the minute they break out.

CONSOLIDATIONS: A TEXTBOOK DEFINITION

Let's define a *market consolidation*. A dictionary definition is as follows: "The world of commercial activity where goods and services are bought and sold; without competition there would be no market." A dictionary definition of a *consolidation* is "something that has consolidated into a compact mass; combining into a solid mass; an occurrence that results in things being united."

Reading these two textbook definitions leads one to believe that a market consolidation is a phenomenon in which the competition between buyers and sellers unites to form a compact mass. Now, how about a look at a trader's definition of a market consolidation? Traders say that, in a consolidation, prices have remained range bound within a narrow price channel.

Is market consolidation an area where little or no new information has come into the market to cause great disagreement concerning the value or perceived value that might move prices? And do trends occur because the value or perceived value is changing so much that the price must change to represent the new value?

Answering "yes" to these questions leads to the conclusion that market consolidations are areas where no new value perceptions are being generated. Thus, prices remain "tight" or range bound.

THE NATURE OR PSYCHOLOGY OF BRACKETED MARKETS

Bracketed markets, by their very nature, cannot last forever because they become increasingly unstable with time. Most traders view a bracketed market as a stabilization of price, but this type of market actually becomes increasingly unstable with time. In fact, the longer a market remains bracketed, the more unstable it becomes.

Bracketed markets and market consolidations have their own cycles. During their initial formation, traders are undecided as to value, and the price oscillates. If this condition continues, traders' perceptions of this asset's value remain the same until new information enters the market to change those perceptions.

Until new information arrives, the consolidation becomes narrower and narrower—to a point where the consolidation is now very unstable; this is where new trends are born.

The longer or more mature the consolidation is, the more significant the new trend following that consolidation will be. Lengthy (or mature) bracketed markets are so unstable that even just a whisper of new information coming into this type of market can make it move, but a shout of information can make it trend fast!

Once you spot a mature consolidated market, your trading approach should be to bracket the upper and lower part of the consolidation. This helps you avoid unprofitable "whipsawing" trades within the consolidation channel caused by insignificant trading reactions from minor market information. It is important that your trading approach does not react to every "whisper" of information that the market ultimately finds meaningless.

FINDING AND MONITORING BRACKETED MARKETS

The first step in this process is to find markets that are bracketed, so you can be ready to trade the breakout when it occurs. To find these consolidated and bracketed markets, it will be best to scan for markets with low volatility and narrow price movement. Look for a consolidation with at least 20 price bars before considering it for a potential trade based on bracketing the high and low of the channel.

Because markets can consolidate for weeks and even months, you will want to monitor several markets simultaneously while they are in consolidation; this way, you do not have to wait a long time before entering a trade. For day traders, significant market consolidations can last from 20 minutes to hours depending on the intraday time frame you choose.

MEASURING THE LENGTH OF BRACKETED MARKETS

Once you have identified a bracketed market of at least 20 price bars, the next thing to do is to draw a line at the top and bottom of the consolidation channel, effectively bracketing the consolidation. Then, place your long trade entry one tick above the upper consolidation band and your short trade entry one tick below the lower consolidation band. When the market breaks the bracket and begins to trend, your first trend trade entry can be taken on the first Pyramid Trading Point that forms. An initial stop loss is set as on the base leg of the Pyramid Trading Point as you would normally do.

Active traders can use this technique to scan for trade setups, and, with 9,000+ stocks, the trader can be quite active! If you're a day trader, you can scan intraday charts looking for consolidations as well. Be sure to go to www.worden.com for some terrific scanning software. For more information, refer to Appendix D.

ALTERNATE EXIT STRATEGY

The alternate exit strategy can be used instead of the Pyramid Trading Point base leg trade exit in which you exit the market as prices move one tick to the other side of the base leg.

With this alternate strategy you wait for prices to *close* on the other side of the Pyramid Trading Point's base leg. The difference is to wait for the price bar's close to make the determination to exit the market. This alternate exit strategy can be beneficial by avoiding unnecessary market exits based on quick temporary selling pressure.

Figure 26.1 illustrates the alternate exit strategy.

USING BRACKETED MARKETS TO TREND TRADE

In trend trading, you make money from catching a significant trend. Money lost in trading occurs by missing or being on the wrong side of trends. So the real question is, "How do we protect and preserve our trading capital as we position ourselves to catch the next profitable trend?"

Significant trends are known to emerge from market consolidations and brackets, and it is during these consolidations that traders experience whipsawing. This phenomenon leads to psychological trauma that can cause havoc with a trader's life, which can, in turn, cause the trader to miss the trend altogether!

It is said that markets trend approximately 35 percent of the time, meaning that 65 percent of the time they are trendless. Consolidations are known to occur before many significant market trends, and, to be a profitable trader, you must learn how to exploit these trends while not losing your money when the market is trendless.

By bracketing your trade entries above and below the consolidation channel, you automatically eliminate unnecessary losing trades. If you

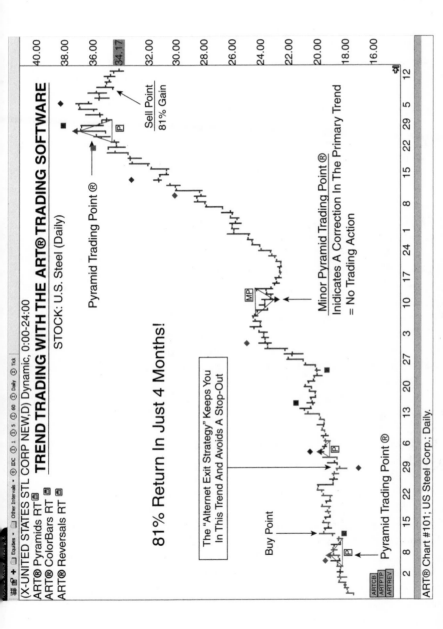

FIGURE 26.1 Alternate Exit Strategy Prevents an Unnecessary Stop-Loss Exit
Source: eSignal. www.eSignal.com

are an aggressive trader who welcomes the additional risk of a few losing trades within the channel to achieve a superior trade entry price, you should wait for the mature consolidation to get very tight and thus very unstable.

This will increase your odds of successfully timing the next significant trend and, therefore, reward your aggressive entry approach. Just as important as the length of time of the consolidation is the low average true range or volatility of prices in recognizing the mature end of the consolidation before a significant new tend emerges.

It is important to note that not all significant trends emerge only from market consolidations. But, if you recognize a consolidation in the market, the potential is great for a significant trend to emerge.

USING THE ART SOFTWARE TO DEFINE BRACKETED MARKETS

The ART software can automatically define a bracketed market that is in consolidation using Pyramid Trading Points. The ART software usually brackets market consolidations with yellow unconfirmed Pyramid Trading Points as illustrated in Figure 26.3.

The apex of tops of the triangle Pyramid Trading Points will determine the top and bottom of the market consolidation and outline the channel of resistance and support levels similar to when you manually draw in the top and bottom lines of the market consolidation.

MANUALLY IDENTIFYING BRACKETED MARKETS

There are times when the volatility within a bracketed market consolidation is such that the ART software is unable to use yellow unconfirmed Pyramid Trading Points to identify the consolidation. When this occurs, the solution is to manually draw a line representing the high of the channel known as a *key level of resistance*, and also draw a line on the low of the channel known as a *key level of support*. Drawing these lines of resistance and support make it easy to identify the upper and lower levels of the market consolidation.

The stock chart in Figure 26.2 subsequently illustrates a market consolidation in Nortel's stock, with upper and lower lines drawn in that identify the market consolidation.

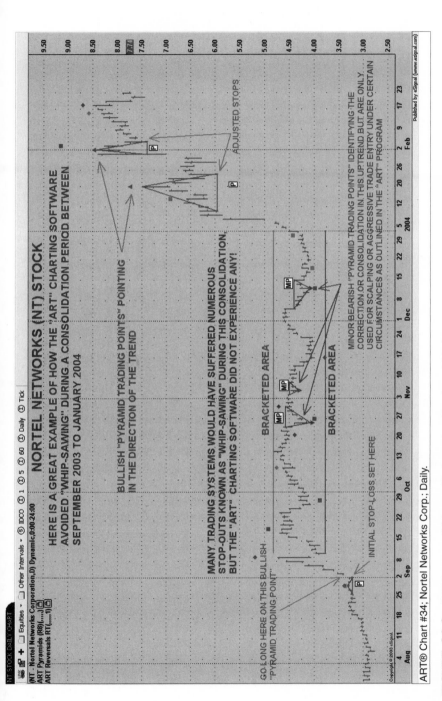

FIGURE 26.2 ART Prevents Whipsaw Madness in a Bracketed Market
Source: eSignal. www.eSignal.com

173

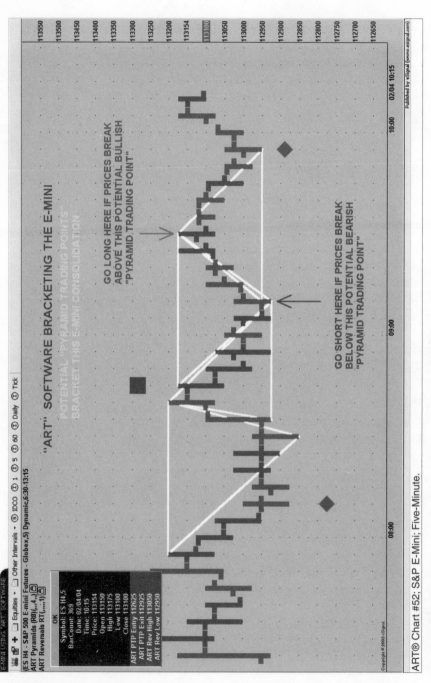

FIGURE 26.3 ART Shows Yellow Potential Pyramid Trading Points in a Bracketed Market

Source: eSignal. www.eSignal.com

Note how prices become even more compressed toward the end of the consolidation, just before this market begins to trend. This occurs often because markets usually spring from compressed price consolidation.

When the market finally breaks above the channel, you should enter your trade one tick above the upper, green-colored band or line (as seen in Figure 26.2). Your initial stop loss is placed one tick under the lower band and adjusted upward as market activity warrants.

SCALPING BRACKETED MARKETS

Scalpers also love bracketed market consolidations. Using the ART Reversals, you can scalp between the high and low of the market channel. This "scalping" technique involves waiting for an ART Reversal to form within 3 percent of the high and low resistance and support lines representing the highs and lows of the market channel.

It is important that the market channel be wide enough to allow enough room or spread in prices in order to make a profit worthy enough in relation to the risk.

You can also scalp the market channel while waiting for the breakout and then begin to trend trade the breakout. So, in effect, you are using two different styles of trading and adapting which style to use according to market conditions yet also maintaining strict risk control on each trade.

USING OPTIONS ON BRACKETED MARKETS

Bracketed market consolidations are also excellent opportunities to bracket the market using option spreads, where your profit is realized from the time decay of the option premium, which occurs if the market channel is long enough.

When the market breaks the consolidation, the option spread then must be adjusted to lock in profit and make money from the developing trend. With this technique, you wait until the market consolidates on the time frame of your choice. You can even monitor many different charts and time frames waiting for a nice consolidation to occur. Large trends usually develop from consolidating markets.

Note: The longer the consolidation/bracket, usually the bigger the upcoming trend will be.

And it does not matter which way the market breaks because you will bracket the market trade in the direction of the break above or below

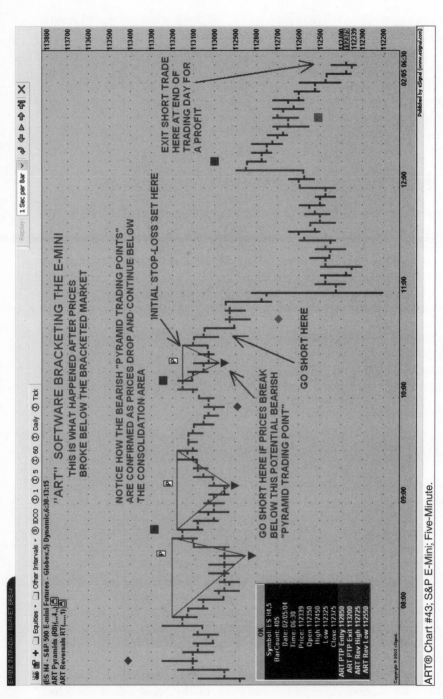

FIGURE 26.4 When the Market Breaks to the Downside, the Bearish Triangles Are Confirmed and Turn Red; the Yellow Bullish Triangles Disappear

Source: eSignal. www.eSignal.com

consolidation. Figure 26.3 is an e-mini five-minute intraday chart illustrating how the ART charting software bracketed this consolidation. Now let's see what happened. Figure 26.4 shows the same e-mini intraday chart at the end of the trading day and after the market broke below consolidation.

Spotting consolidation areas can be a powerful way to get in on new trends. Remember, the longer the market stays in consolidation usually means the bigger the new trend will be when the market breaks consolidation.

CHAPTER 27

Software Optimization and Average True Range (ATR)

Adjusting the ART Trading Software to take advantage of a market's volatility as measured by the average true range (ATR) of price bars will help reduce losses on certain market cycles.

Using ART trading software, you can change and optimize the settings as outlined in the *ART Charting Software User's Manual*. The default settings usually work well on most market scenarios, but there are times when an increase in volatility requires an adjustment.

Both the ART Pyramids and the ART Reversals can be adjusted or "optimized." You may need to make software-optimizing adjustments when changing time frames and markets.

DETERMINE VOLATILITY USING ATR

Some drawdown periods are a result of an increase in market volatility that can be lessened by optimizing your software. You can determine volatility by using the ATR indicator, which is useful when optimizing the ART trading software.

ATR measures volatility based on a price bar's length, but not on price swing movement volatility. In other words, the ATR will increase if the price bar's length increases but does not measure beyond that.

This means that if you have a price movement from, let's say, 5 to 20 made up of 10 price bars of equal length but all moving upward, the ATR in this example would remain the same. This indicates no change in volatility because the price bar's length remained constant.

If, however, in this same example, you had an increase in the price bar's length so it took only 6 price bars to travel the distance, then the ATR would increase indicating increasing volatility.

What is important with the Pyramid Trading Point optimization settings is what we call the market's "swing volatility." You can experience volatility without experiencing a change in a price bar's length, and the ATR would not indicate this increase in volatility.

This is why you do not use ATR alone to determine a change in Pyramid Trading Point optimization. Instead, use a trend-line channel to measure the valleys versus the peaks.

The wider the channel, the higher the volatility and the need to change the optimization based on this current trend only. Once the trend is over, change the optimization back to its default and change it again only if a new trend channel becomes wider.

Using this method you will not be overoptimizing. You do have to wait until you have determined that a trend is in place by being able to draw a trend channel after a few Pyramid Trading Points fail.

Some traders optimize their software based on best results from a given market's history.

When optimizing ART Reversal bars, these signals occur when extremes exist in the market caused by fear and greed. These reversals are usually best when they appear after a steep rise or fall in the market when emotions are high.

When optimizing ART Reversals, a "stricter" setting will result in fewer ART Reversals trades, but those trades will occur at significant emotional levels in the market and should be some of your best trades.

How you optimize the software is part of the ART of trading and you will need to practice this through paper-trading to determine your profitability.

RULES FOR ART SOFTWARE OPTIMIZATION

These are helpful rules when you are trying to determine the best time frame and markets to trade. When first looking at a new market, it is important to try and match the ART trading software to that market. When looking at a new market and time frame, there are two quick checks you can do to see if the software is matched to that market:

1. Adjust the ART trading software MinScore or MinFormScore until you see the most profitable trades for your style of trading.
2. Change time frames until the ART trading software until you see the most profitable trades for your style of trading.

If neither works, you can change markets and come back to it when the market cycle improves and is favorable to your style of trading.

CHAPTER 28

Stop and Reverse (SAR)

T he meaning of stop and reverse (SAR) is that you change the direction of your trade immediately without going to a neutral or flat position. This needs to be done quickly, deliberately, and without hesitation. You should know that a potential SAR is developing and be ready to execute it. This is an advanced technique.

SARs create a lot of trading. When you are trying SARs for the first time, you will be surprised at how many extra trades were done as compared to not using SARs. You will also be surprised at how much more you have to pay in commission. SARs are not for everyone! You must know what you can tolerate before using SARs. Try paper-trading and see how you feel. You will know pretty quickly if using SARs is for you.

A great SAR pattern is the ART One-Bar Reversal. For example, you are long stock XYZ or futures contract X and the market has been trending in your favor nicely. Then, all of a sudden, an ART One-Bar Reversal develops.

You have two options: Either exit the long trade if prices fall one tick below the ART One-Bar Reversal bar or do an SAR and exit all long positions one tick under the ART One-Bar Reversal, and also go immediately short. The new initial stop loss for the short position is now one tick above the ART One-Bar Reversal bar. Other SARs can be taken off a Two-Bar Reversal pattern.

You will make money if the correction is strong enough to cause a significant pullback. Of course, the uptrend may be so strong that the new buyers come in immediately after a slight correction and drive prices upward. That is the risk!

The art in SAR trading is to be sure the volume is high enough to warrant the trade. High volume indicates that other traders are taking profits, too, and the reversal bar indicates more selling than buying. This creates a potential top in the uptrend. The opposite is true for the reverse scenario of a downtrend and trading the correction to the upside using an SAR.

REENTRY PATTERNS

Reentry patterns are more conservative than SARs. Reentry patterns indicate that you were stopped out of the market and are now looking to get back in or reenter the market. Unlike SARs, you are not long or short, but instead "flat," waiting to reenter the same market again.

Perhaps you were stopped out on an ART One-Bar Reversal and that same high-volume bar ends up being a Pyramid Trading Point that can be used to reenter the market. The Pyramid Trading Point is the most common pattern used for reentries.

Another, more aggressive approach is to enter once a correction in an uptrend is over by looking for an ART One-Bar Reversal at the bottom of the correction. Enter the long trade one tick over the top of the ART One-Bar Reversal or the ART Two-Bar Reversal pattern. This can be used for downtrends, but it is done in the opposite way.

THE DIFFERENCE BETWEEN SARs AND REENTRY PATTERNS

SAR trades require confidence and a fearless approach to trading. When you have a few SARs in a row lose money, that will be the test to see how you feel. If you feel nervous or anxious and upset, avoid trading the SARs.

If you are a day trader and, at the end of the day, you feel you have overtraded, avoid using the SAR for a while. If you're day trading, SARs can really run up your commissions, which is okay when you are profitable, but can be devastating if you are not profitable. If you had an unprofitable day trading SARs, and your loss falls within normal drawdown days, you are going to feel okay. But if your SARs cause your drawdown days to be out of line with your normal drawdown days, then stop and reevaluate.

Usually, problems with SARs center around not waiting for high enough volume, signaling a significant turnaround point in the current trend.

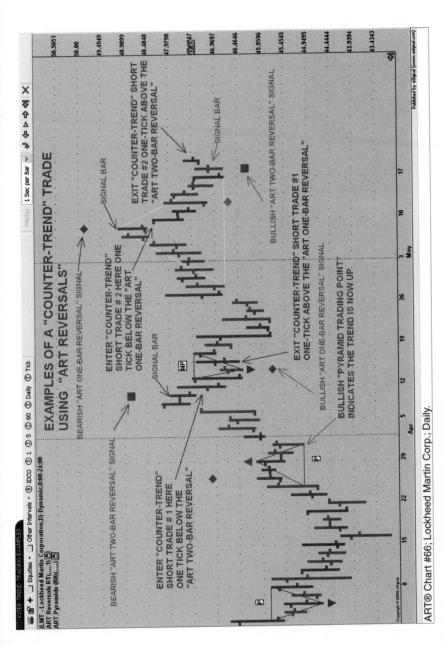

FIGURE 28.1 Countertrend Trades Using ART

Source: eSignal. www.eSignal.com

TRADING BETWEEN ART REVERSAL BAR SIGNALS

There are countless ways to trade ART. How you mix and match trading signals will be determined in part by your beliefs and psychology. You may trade between the ART Reversal bars, and the combinations here are great as well. If you always want to be in the market, you will use SAR orders for every signal, for example, if your first trade is going long on the first bullish ART Reversal and SAR on first following bearish ART Reversal, and so on.

You may decide you will only trade ART Reversals in the direction of the trend as determined by a primary Pyramid Trading Point labeled "P" by the software. Or perhaps you will only trade the ART One-Bar Reversals, or the ART Two-Bar Reversals. Or you can trade none of them and just use the Pyramid Trading Point. If you're a countertrend trader, you may choose to trade against the trend using ART Reversals.

Figure 28.1 is an example of countertrend trading using ART Reversals.

CHAPTER 29

Higher-Time-Frame Filter

Don't filter trades just to be seeking the "Holy Grail." In the final analysis, you may decide to let go and not use filters at all. Be sure your filters do not cause you to form strong opinions that override your risk control discipline. Instead, use filters to confirm the ART trading signals.

Over time, the Pyramid Trading Point captures major trends and, combined with sound money management, is all you need. The challenge is during drawdown when it seems that you are being stopped out often and need to filter your trades. During these drawdowns, your psychology will be tested.

Needing filters can be an illusion. Even while using filters, you will experience drawdown. However, short 1- to 5-minute intraday time frames are especially influenced by traders of higher time frames. Therefore, trading systems can be subject to losses more frequently due to trading activity outside their time frame, which they cannot see or measure. In this case, filters can be beneficial.

The short time frames are the hardest to trade because price patterns that develop among traders in that time frame can be offset by trading on higher time frames. Filters are useful especially on these short time frames. Trade only in the direction of the trend based on a higher time frame: Big profitable trends occur when many different types of traders and investors from many time frames are participating in a trend.

So in trends where the potential exists that many traders will participate you have a stronger trend. Look for entry opportunities that correspond to entries on several time frames. This way, you may have many traders getting in and fueling a significant trend.

No matter what time frame you are trading, this technique can be used. If you're a day trader, swing trader, or an investor, you can use this trading technique. Significant trends involve traders and investors from many time frames trading in the same market direction.

TIME FRAMES TO TRACK THE TREND USING THE HIGHER-TIME-FRAME FILTER

The following list of time frames will help you in determining how to use the higher-time-frame filter.

- 1-minute chart trading: Use the 5-minute chart for trend lines.
- 3-minute chart trading: Use the 10-minute chart for trend lines.
- 5-minute chart trading: Use the 15-minute chart for trend lines.
- 10-minute chart trading: Use the 20-minute chart for trend lines.
- 15-minute chart trading: Use the 30-minute chart for trend lines.
- 20-minute chart trading: Use the 40-minute chart for trend lines.
- 25-minute chart trading: Use the 50-minute chart for trend lines.
- 30-minute chart trading: Use the 60-minute chart for trend lines.
- 35-minute chart trading: Use the 60-minute chart for trend lines.
- 40-minute chart trading: Use the 60-minute chart for trend lines.
- 60-minute chart trading: Use the daily chart for trend lines.
- Daily chart trading: Use the weekly chart for trend lines.
- Weekly chart trading: Use the monthly chart for trend lines.
- Monthly chart trading: Use the quarterly chart for trend lines.

There will be times when the trend is not clear on the time frame you are trading. This is when you need to use the higher-time-frame method. These time frames and their correlation are what I suggest to capture the most current underlying trend.

Note: Some traders may be looking for a more significant trend. In this case, move two time frames out.

USING TREND LINES AND THE HIGHER-TIME-FRAME FILTER

This is a good technique for those who like to trade with the *overall* trend, which may or may not be as clear on the current time frame you are trading.

Use either a simple trend line or a regression trend channel. Instead of using it on the current time frame that you are basing your entries and exits on, use it on a time frame higher.

Figure 29.1 on page 190 shows how to use a higher time frame for trend identification. In this example, the daily stock chart of Applied Materials (AMAT) appears on the left and the weekly chart on the right. The weekly chart is used to determine the immediate trend and the daily chart is used to time your trades in the direction of the weekly chart's trend.

Figure 29.2 on page 191 illustrates how to use higher time frames for day trading. Using a 5-minute time frame to filter trade entries on a 1-minute time frame may be helpful to gauge which trades may be most profitable.

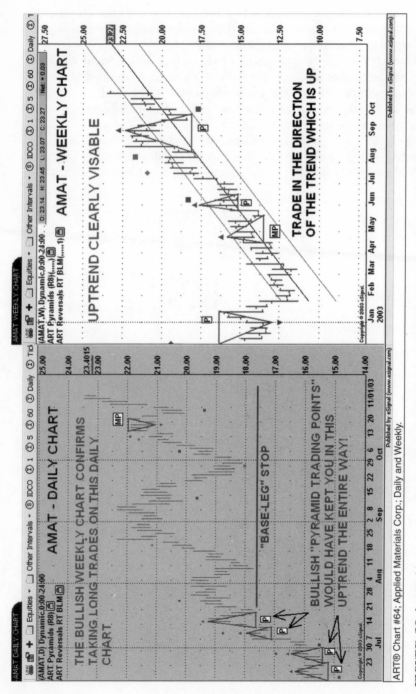

FIGURE 29.1 Weekly Is Used to Determine the Immediate Trend; Daily Is Used to Time the Trade Using the Higher-Time-Frame Filter

ART® Chart #64; Applied Materials Corp.; Daily and Weekly.

Source: eSignal. www.eSignal.com

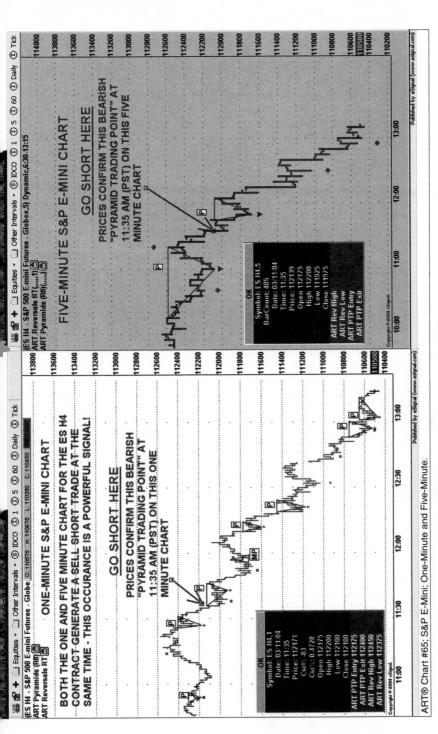

FIGURE 29.2 5-Minute Is Used to Determine the Immediate Trend; 1-Minute Is Used to Time the Trade Using the Higher-Time-Frame Filter

Source: eSignal. www.eSignal.com

191

S&P E-MINI DAY-TRADING EXAMPLES USING THE HIGHER-TIME-FRAME FILTER

The following figures 29.3 through 29.8 show examples of using the ART higher time-frame approach to day trade the S&P e-mini. But remember, this ART technique can be used on any time frame and on any market by day traders, position traders, and investors.

These examples of using multiple time frames show you how to increase your profitability.

EXAMPLE A

Wednesday, February 9, 2005

7:10 AM (PST)   Figure 29.3 shows the S&P e-mini (ES H5) higher-time-frame 10-minute chart:

Trend is down at 7:10 AM (PST) on this higher-time-frame chart.
Enter short trades only on the lower-time-frame chart.

7:50 AM (PST)   Figure 29.4 shows the S&P e-mini (ES H5) lower-time-frame 1-minute chart:

Entry at 7:11 AM (PST).
Exit at 7:50 AM (PST) for a nice profit.

Continue to look for short-trades on the 1-minute chart (as long as the higher-time-frame 10-minute chart trend remains bearish).

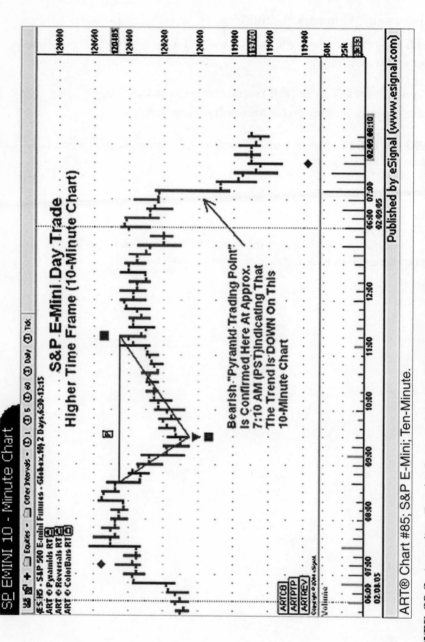

FIGURE 29.3 Immediate Trend Is Down at 7:10 AM (PST) on Higher-Time-Frame 10-Minute Chart
Source: eSignal. www.eSignal.com

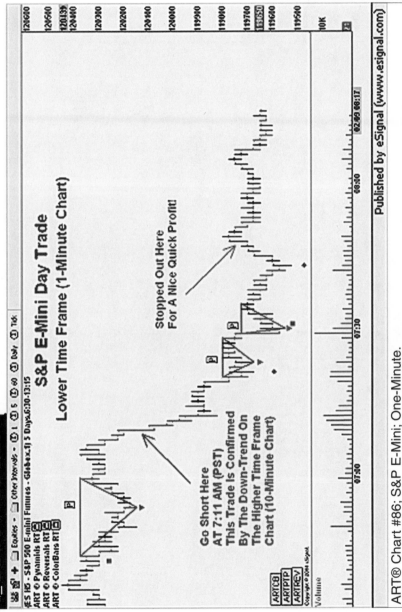

FIGURE 29.4 Entry at 7:11 AM (PST) and Exit at 7:50 AM (PST) on Lower-Time-Frame 1-Minute Chart Using the Primary Pyramid Trading Point Signals

Source: eSignal. www.eSignal.com

EXAMPLE B

Wednesday, February 9, 2005

11:30 AM (PST)   Trend remains down at 11:30 AM (PST) in Figure 29.5. Enter short trades only on the lower-time-frame chart.

11:36 AM (PST)   Figure 29.6 shows the S&P e-mini (ES H5) lower-time-frame 1-minute chart:

Entry at 11:01 AM (PST).

Exit at 11:36 AM (PST) for a nice profit.

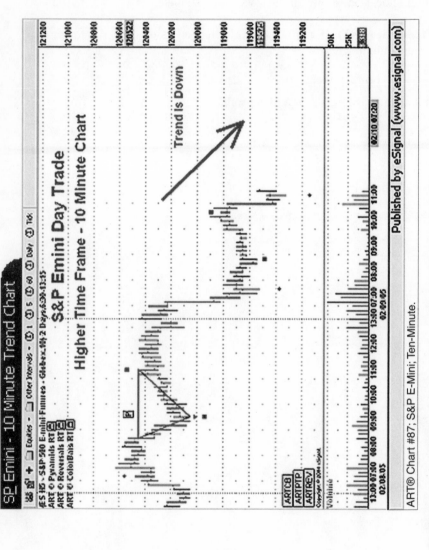

FIGURE 29.5 Immediate Trend Is Down at 11:30 AM (PST) on Higher-Time-Frame 10-Minute Chart
Source: eSignal. www.eSignal.com

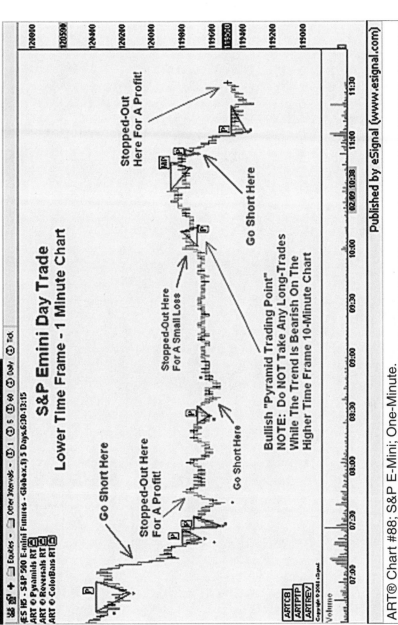

FIGURE 29.6 Entry at 11:01 AM (PST) and Exit at 11:36 AM (PST) On Lower-Time-Frame 1-Minute Chart Using the Primary Pyramid Trading Point Signals
Source: eSignal. www.eSignal.com

199

EXAMPLE C

Wednesday, February 9, 2005

After the Close   Figure 29.7 shows that the trend remained down throughout the trading day on the higher 10-minute chart. Look for short trades only on the lower-time-frame chart.

12:50 PM (PST)   Figure 29.8 shows that trading with the trend on a higher time frame allowed only short trades.

S&P e-mini (ES H5) lower-time-frame 1-minute chart:

Entry at 12:50 PM (PST).

Exit near close of market for a small profit.

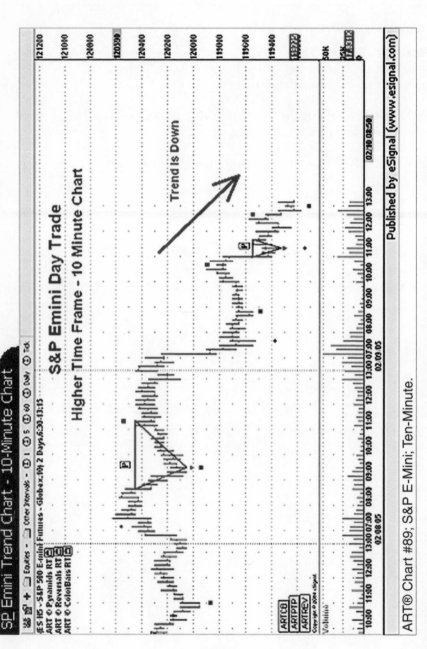

FIGURE 29.7 Immediate Trend Is Down at 12:00 PM (PST) on Higher-Time-Frame 10-Minute Chart

Source: eSignal. www.eSignal.com

ART® Chart #89; S&P E-Mini; Ten-Minute.

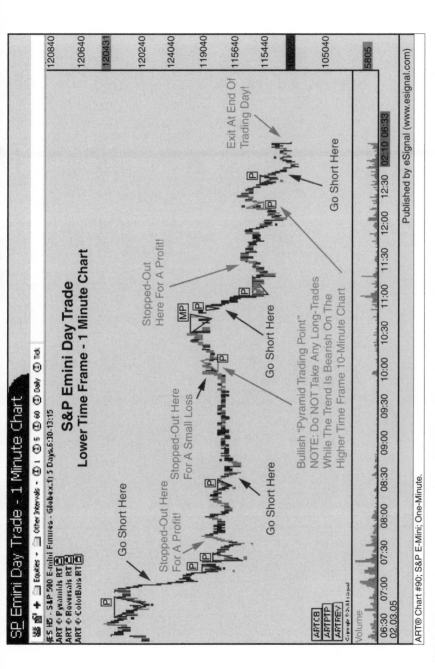

FIGURE 29.8 Entry at 12:50 PM (PST) and Exit at Close of Market 1:00 PM (PST) Using the Primary Pyramid Trading Point Signals
Source: eSignal. www.eSignal.com

CHAPTER 30

Other Filter Techniques

T his chapter has a variety of popular filters that can be used with the ART software. Remember that these filters are not the "Holy Grail" and are not required to be profitable using the ART software. They are listed here to give you some advanced techniques to experiment with after you have mastered the ART basics. Be sure to paper-trade these techniques prior to going live in the market.

FILTER FOR TRADING THE E-MINI

Use the spread between the NQ contract and the ES contract as a means to help confirm ART trading signals: An increasing spread confirms an up-trend, while a decreasing spread confirms a downtrend. Spreads are represented on a chart with a line instead of individual price bars. Enter trades only when confirmed by the spread. A spread goes up as the Nasdaq index (NQ) outperforms the S&P index (ES).

In a bullish market environment, money flows faster into high-growth companies as represented by the Nasdaq market, and thus the spread increases upward. In a poor market environment, money flows faster into the safer S&P stocks, and thus the spread decreases downward.

For lower time frames like the 1-minute intraday periods, you may want to try using a higher time frame like a 5-minute or 15-minute spread; 1-, 3-, and 5-minute spreads can at times be too sensitive and therefore jump around too much to be helpful.

Figure 30.1 illustrates how the NQ-ES spread can work.

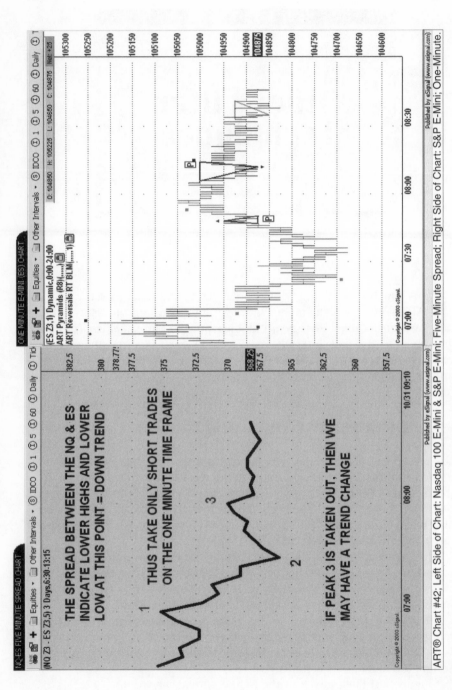

FIGURE 30.1 Using The NQ-ES Spread to Confirm ART Signals

Source: eSignal. www.eSignal.com

ACCUMULATION/DISTRIBUTION

Charting platforms usually have this as a standard indicator. In using this, you are not forecasting but confirming ART signals. Figure 30.2 illustrates how to use accumulation/distribution to confirm the ART signals.

USING ON-BALANCE VOLUME (OBV)

Most charting platforms usually have this as a standard indicator. In using this, you are not forecasting but confirming ART trading signals. Figure 30.3 illustrates how to use OBV to confirm the ART signals.

PRICE OSCILLATOR HISTOGRAM

Price oscillators are usually standard with most charting platforms. They can be used to confirm ART trading signals. Figure 30.4 illustrates how we use the price oscillator histogram to confirm the ART signals. Figure 30.5 is another chart illustrating how you can use the price oscillator histogram to confirm the ART signals.

PRICE OSCILLATOR HISTOGRAM SETTINGS

1. Short length to 5
2. Long length to 35
3. Source to low
4. Set to "histogram"

When using the price oscillator histogram as a filter, there are four ART methods:

1. **A.** *Go long* when the histogram is increasing relative to its previous histogram bar at the time of an ART trade entry.

   B. *Go short* when the histogram is decreasing relative to its previous histogram bar at the time of an ART trade entry.
2. **A.** *Go long* when the histogram is above the zero line and increasing relative to its previous histogram bar at the time when prices are triggering a trade entry.

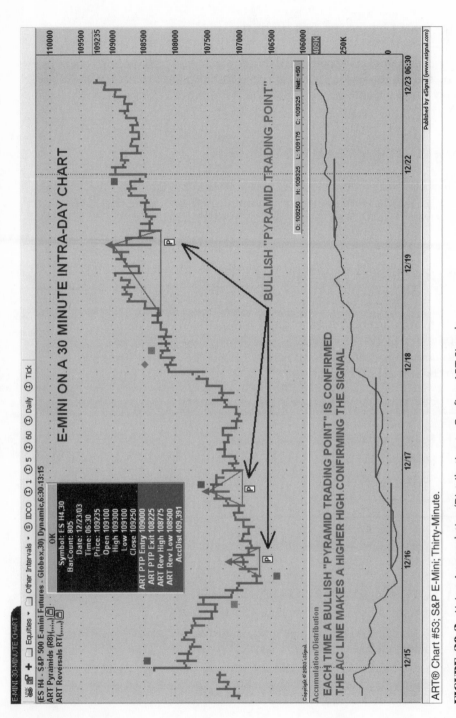

ART® Chart #53; S&P E-Mini; Thirty-Minute.

FIGURE 30.2 Using Accumulation/Distribution to Confirm ART Signals

Source: eSignal. www.eSignal.com

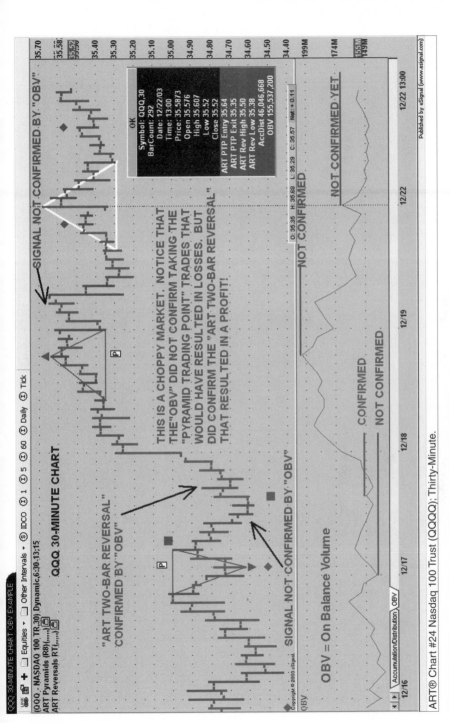

ART® Chart #24 Nasdaq 100 Trust (QQQQ); Thirty-Minute.

FIGURE 30.3 Using On-Balance Volume to Confirm ART Signals

Source: eSignal. www.eSignal.com

209

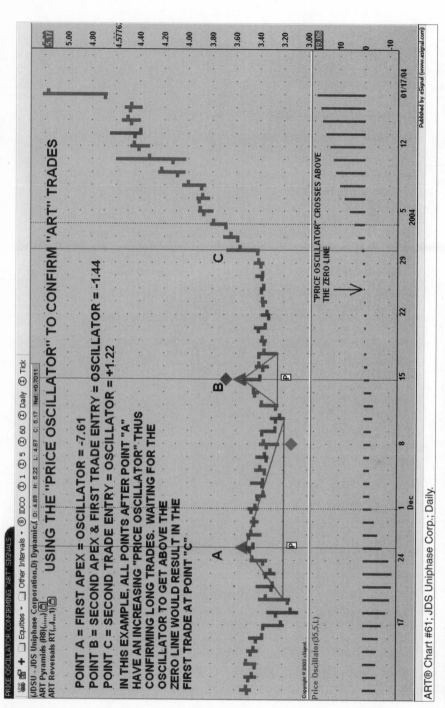

FIGURE 30.4 Using Price Oscillator Histogram to Confirm ART Signals
Source: eSignal. www.eSignal.com

210

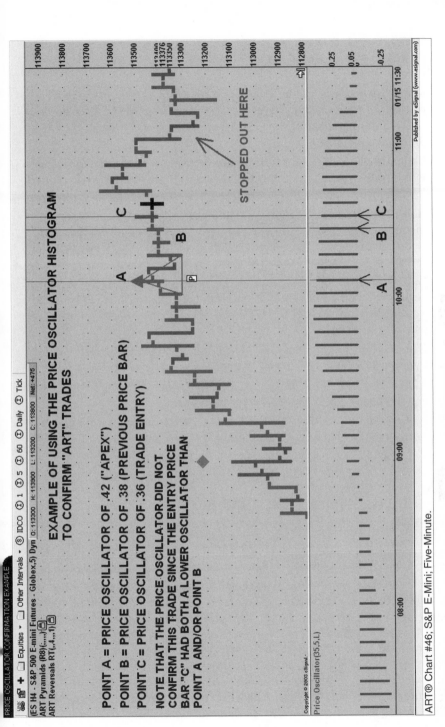

FIGURE 30.5 Using Price Oscillator Histogram to Confirm ART Signals
Source: eSignal. www.eSignal.com

B. *Go short* when the histogram is below the zero line and decreasing relative to its previous bar at the time when prices are triggering a trade entry.

Note: You may miss some great early trades in a new emerging trend if you wait for the oscillator to get on the correct side of the zero line before taking trades. However, if you like more confirmation you will prefer this technique.

3. Compare the histogram of the signal bar (apex of a Pyramid Trading Point, or the signal bar of an ART Reversal) to that of the histogram at the time when market prices are triggering a trade entry.

A. *Go long:* If the histogram at the point of a trade entry is greater than the histogram at either the apex of the bullish Pyramid Trading Point or an ART Reversal bar signal bar, then go long. Otherwise, pass on the trade.

B. *Go short:* If the histogram at the point of a trade entry is more negative than the histogram at either the apex of the bearish Pyramid Trading Point or an ART Reversal bar signal, then go short. Otherwise, pass on the trade.

4. Exits: The histogram can also be used in conjunction with the minor Pyramid Trading Point labeled MP for exiting the market.

A. *In a long position:* Exit if a bearish MP Pyramid Trading Point forms and the histogram is also below the zero line.

B. *In a short position:* Exit if a bullish MP Pyramid Trading Point forms and the histogram is also above the zero line.

TRADE ONLY AFTER THREE CONSECUTIVE LOSSES

This technique of trading after three consecutive losses is unique and easy to use. Wait for at least three consecutive losses in a row before entering a new trade. You want to increase your win ratio by stacking the odds in your favor that the next trade you enter will be a winner. If you wait for at least three trades to end in losses, then the probabilities are now in your favor for the next trade to be a winner.

You must realize that you will trade less frequently and may miss some great trades while waiting for at least three consecutive losses to occur. However, you may even want to wait for a rare four losses in a row if you want to really increase the probabilities on the next trade. Using this technique should limit your drawdown periods substantially.

TRADE IN THE DIRECTION OF YOUR FORECASTING METHOD

If you use this filter, then it is best that you use the Elliott Wave as your fore-casting "tool." Then you need to decide if you want to apply this forecasting tool to the current time frame you are trading, one higher time frame, or both. Again, if you want to go this route, paper-trade until you become an expert at combining your forecasting tool with ART.

CHAPTER 31

Elliott Wave—
Ungrounded
Assessment

T he Elliott Wave (EW) theory is the most powerful forecasting tool I know of. The EW theory takes into account world, economic, and behavioral aspects of the environment. World events like war, economic depressions, and acts of God (e.g., earthquakes and weather disasters) consistently fall into the wave sequence. This makes the wave sequence valid as a forecasting tool. Don't ask me how it does it; just know that I have witnessed this occurrence time and time again, including the sell-off starting in the year 2000 and the recovery beginning in 2003.

With this said, it is important for me to mention that I do believe in the EW as a measure of human reactions. The EW effectively represents how humans emotionally respond to world and economic events in the markets. But remember, until the EW actually occurs, thinking or forecasting that it might occur is only a fantasy or theory.

EW patterns are not needed to trade successfully. It is much better to flow with the market and trade the realities of the market. In other words, if the trend is up, stay with the trend until it actually changes, regardless of what the EW is forecasting

Figure 31.1 was created in December 2003 after the probability of an EW 4 bottom was hit in March 2003. This chart illustrates how using Fibonacci retracement levels in combination with the EW verifies the bottom.

This allows us to apply the EW principles to the next bullish impulsive wave, which should take the Dow Jones Industrial Average (DJIA) to substantial new highs between 2008 and 2010.

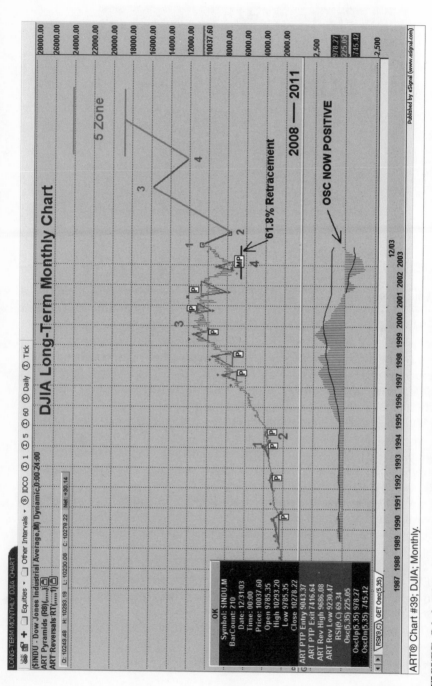

FIGURE 31.1 This chart was created in December 2003 and shows how the Elliott Wave effectively looked into the future and forecasted our recent 2007 new highs in the DJIA

Source: eSignal. www.eSignal.com

216

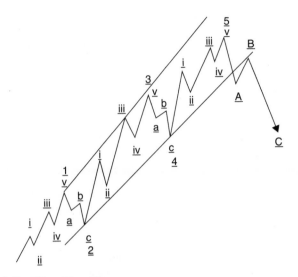

FIGURE 31.2 Elliott Wave Diagram

Knowing how to use the EW can be a very profitable skill. Here are some insights into how you can use the EW with your ART trading approach (*Note:* Waves refer to Elliott Waves). See Figure 31.2.

ELLIOTT WAVE GUIDELINES

1. Tradable waves are impulsive waves 1, 3, 5, and corrective "C" wave (of wave 4 corrections).

2. Impulsive wave 3 is the steepest and most dramatic wave of all the waves and occurs on the highest volume and highest Elliott Wave oscillator (or moving average convergence/divergence [MACD]) of all waves. Wave 3 is never the shortest wave.

3. Waves 1, 3, and 5 are made up of five minor waves and most corrections are a-b-c corrections. Irregular corrective waves exist.

4. Wave 5 will usually exceed wave 3 on lower volume than the wave 3 high.

5. Wave 5 can fail and just form a double top with Wave 3 instead of going to higher price levels.

6. Always base your trade entries and exits using ART grounded assessment trading signals.

7. Most traders get whipsawed and lose money in wave 4. Don't assume wave 4 is over until you can clearly see an a-b-c wave pattern with

the correction ending 38 percent to 61.8 percent between wave 2 and wave 3. Wave B is usually 50 percent of wave A and should not exceed 75 percent of wave A. Wave C is 1 × wave A or 1.62 × wave A or 2.62 × wave A.

8. If wave 2 is simple, then wave 4 will most likely be complex, and vice versa.

9. Corrective wave 2 statistics: Only 12 percent retrace within 38 percent of wave 1; 73 percent retrace between 50 percent and 60 percent, and 15 percent retrace below 62 percent.

10. Impulsive wave 3 statistics: 45 percent of the time wave 3 reaches 1.6 to 1.75 times wave 1; 30 percent of the time between 1.75 to 2.62 times wave 1; 15 percent of the time between 1.00 to 1.60 times wave 1; and 8 percent of the time greater than 2.62 times wave 1.

11. Corrective wave 4 statistics: 60 percent retrace between 30 percent and 50 percent of wave 3; 15 percent retrace between 24 percent and 30 percent of wave 3; and 15 percent retrace between 50 percent and 62 percent of wave 3.

12. Impulsive wave 5 statistics: Use extended Fibonacci calculations to determine the price zone for wave 5. Wave 5 usually ends between 1.0 and 1.62 times the length of the beginning of wave 1 to the end of wave 3. Failed wave 5s do occur.

13. If you enter a potential wave 5 trade at a wave 4 Fibonacci retracement level (i.e., 38 percent or 50 percent), set your stop somewhere around the 62 percent retracement level because the normal maximum wave 4 retracement level is 61.8 percent. Be sure to adjust your position size accordingly. Then, once you are sure you are in wave 5, add on to your position size using any ART signal that you can.

14. Trade *only* in the direction of waves 1, 3, 5, and C (of wave 4) on the primary time frame that you use to base your entries and exits.

15. To confirm or filter your trades, trade *only* in the direction of waves 1, 3, 5, and C (of wave 4) on the higher time frame of one Fibonacci degree.

16. Wave counts can change, and it is possible at many points to have alternate wave counts. For example, you may think you are in a wave 4 correction until the correction exceeds its maximum retracement level and instead turns into an impulsive wave 3 in the opposite direction! So you must adhere to your stops!

Figure 31.3 is an example of using both grounded and ungrounded trading assessments. See how the Pyramid Trading Point adds structure to Elliott Wave theory.

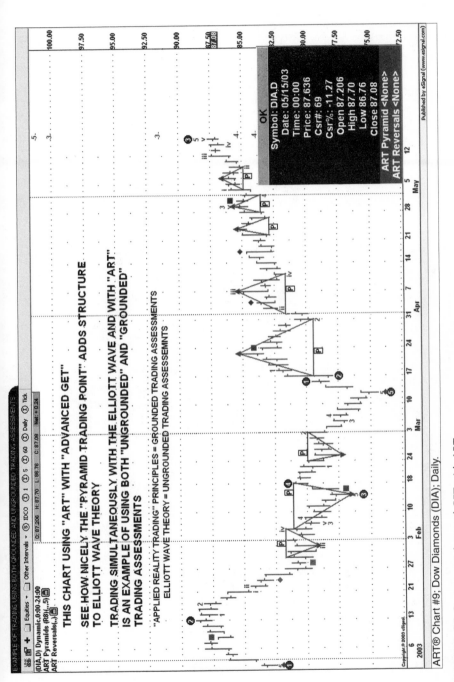

FIGURE 31.3 Using Advanced GET with ART
Source: eSignal. www.eSignal.com

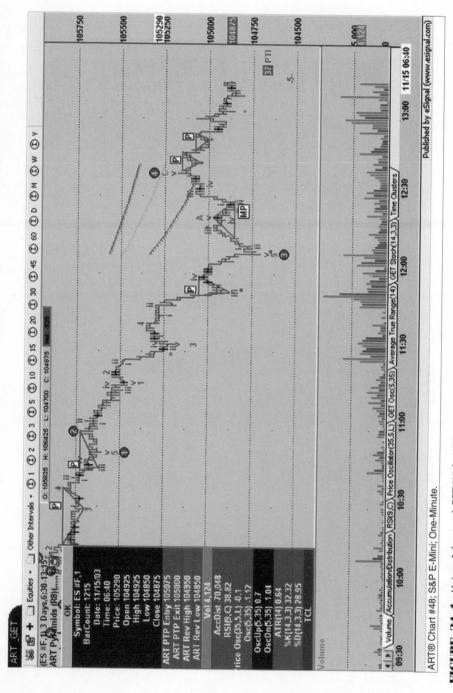

FIGURE 31.4 Using Advanced GET With ART

Source: eSignal. www.eSignal.com

Figure 31.4 shows how Applied Reality Trading adds structure to a forecasting method like the Elliott Wave. On this chart, there clearly is a bearish trend down with the Elliott Waves identifying impulsive and corrective waves. The Pyramid Trading Point adds structure and sound risk control to Elliott Wave trading.

CHAPTER 32

Other Ungrounded Assessments

T here are many ungrounded assessment tools available to you. Following are a list of the most frequently used tools. Keep in mind that you can be a profitable trader without using these advanced techniques. They are provided to you here so that you can experiment to see if these can boost your profitability. Be sure to paper-trade these techniques prior to going into the market live.

PRICE OSCILLATOR HISTOGRAM

Oscillators are derivatives of price and volume and take you further away from the truths of the market. If you have the proper mind-set and are not prone to form opinions based on these tools, then you may use them to your advantage. Beware, they are not the "Holy Grail"!

Price Oscillator Histogram Guidelines

a. Use the Price Oscillator Histogram when counting Elliott Waves (EWs). Price oscillators are standard with most charting platforms.

b. Use these Price Oscillator settings:

Short length to 5

Long length to 35

Source to low

Set to "histogram"

Look for the highest peak of the price oscillator histogram to spot a wave 3 of some degree on your chart

c. Look for divergence at the end of wave 5 or to identify the end of wave 5 in wave 3.

FIBONACCI STUDIES

Fibonacci studies help determine where corrections will end, extensions will end (price targets), and when. Use them alone or in conjunction with the EW theory, and the EW Fibonacci statistics stated in this book. Most charting software comes with instructions on how to use them.

Fibonacci retracements and Fibonacci extensions use horizontal lines to indicate areas of support or resistance. They answer the question of at what price levels will there be significant support or resistance for a change in trend.

Fibonacci time zones answer the question of when will prices reach these significant support and resistance price levels. Fibonacci studies are not intended to provide the primary indications for timing trade entries and exits. Fibonacci studies can be used as a trade confirmation tool, indicating prices have either reached appropriate levels of support or resistance. Fibonacci studies are often used with EWs to predict the extent of the retracements and extensions after waves.

FIBONACCI RETRACEMENTS

Retracements are calculated by first locating the high and low of the chart. Then five horizontal lines are drawn:

1. At 100 percent (the high on the chart)
2. At 61.8 percent
3. At 50 percent
4. At 38.2 percent
5. At 0 percent (the low on the chart)

After a significant price movement up or down, the new support and resistance levels are often at or near these lines.

Figure 32.1 shows that wave 4 potentially could end between 50 percent and 61.8 percent Fibonacci retracement levels as indicated on this chart by the elliptical circle that was drawn in based on Fibonacci levels. As it turned out, this elliptical circle is precisely where prices did end before the next bullish impulsive Elliott Wave 5 began in March 2003.

You may use a price oscillator, which is usually a standard charting feature on most charting platforms. See the "Price Oscillator" section of this chapter to see how to best identify Elliott Wave patterns.

FIBONACCI EXTENSIONS

Extensions are calculated by first locating the last wave high and low. Then five horizontal lines are drawn:

1. At 0 percent (at the end of the corrective wave)
2. At 38.2 percent
3. At 50 percent
4. At 61.8 percent
5. At 100 percent

Like retracements, after a significant price movement up or down, the new support and resistance levels are often at or near these lines.

FIBONACCI TIME ZONES

Unlike the other Fibonacci methods, time zones are a series of vertical lines. They are composed by dividing a chart into segments with vertical lines spaced apart in increments that conform to the Fibonacci sequence (1, 1, 2, 3, 5, 8, 13, etc.). These lines indicate areas in which major price movement can be expected.

Leonardo Fibonacci (1170–1240) of Pisa, Italy, was a thirteenth-century mathematician, and many would say the greatest mathematician of medieval times. He developed the Fibonacci approaches that are used by traders around the world. Fibonacci and Elliott Wave theory are commonly used together and Ralph Nelson Elliott (1871–1948) developed the Elliott Wave theories. The Elliott Wave has time and time again has proven to me to be remarkably effective in "forecasting" the market. You should also study his approach and read a book about Elliott Wave listed in Appendix D.

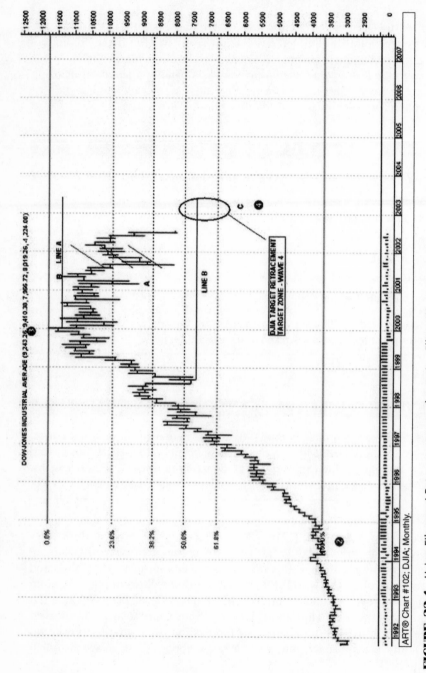

FIGURE 32.1 Using Fibonacci Retracements to determine Elliott Wave correction target zones

Source: www.eSignal.com

RELATIVE STRENGTH INDICATOR (RSI)

ART uses the RSI in a unique way. Look for periods when the RSI peaks above the 80 percent band or below the 20 percent band.

RSI SETTINGS

1. Close length to 9
2. Upper band to 80 percent
3. Lower band to 20 percent

For example, when the RSI:

- Penetrates above the 80 percent band:
  The market is usually making a new significant high and will most likely return—even after a temporary sell off—to take out that market high.
- Penetrates below the 20 percent band:
  The market is usually making a new significant low and will most likely return—even after a temporary rally—to take out that market low.

On a rare occurrence, the RSI can penetrate both the upper and lower bands consecutively without new higher highs or lower lows occurring. When this happens, use the most recent band penetration as your guide.

Figure 32.2 is an example of using RSI to confirm ART trading signals.

This RSI technique is helpful provided you use the ART trading system to manage your trades. You can use this technique to see if the market has made a high-probability significant bottom or top. This is helpful if you want to be aggressive in getting into new trends or selecting an exit on exhausted trends.

Figure 32.3 is an example of using RSI to confirm ART trading signals. Even though there was one time when the RSI technique did not work as expected, the Pyramid Trading Point kept you out of harm's way!

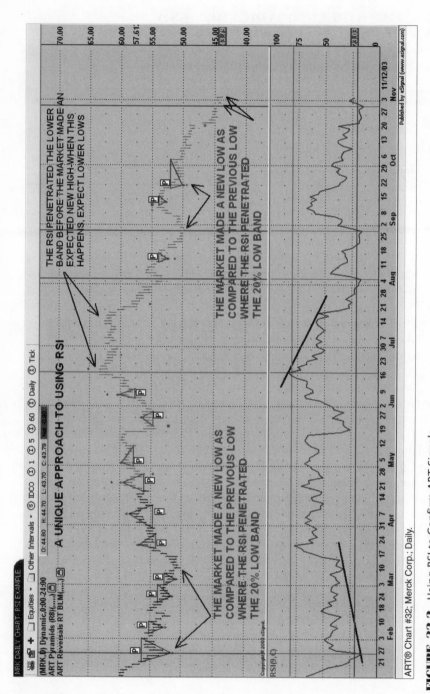

FIGURE 32.2 Using RSI to Confirm ART Signals
Source: eSignal. www.eSignal.com

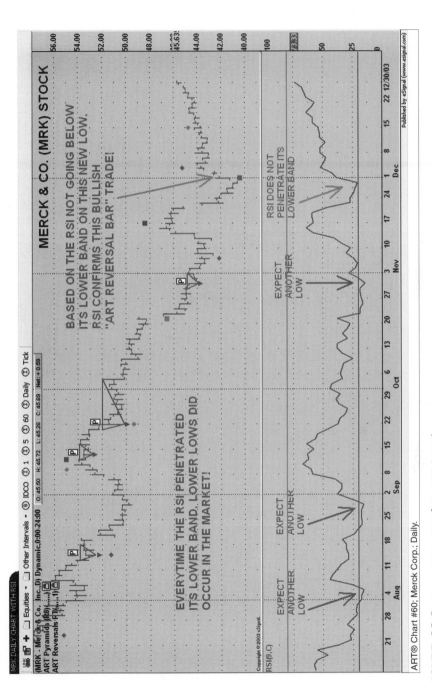

FIGURE 32.3 Using RSI to Confirm ART Signals

Source: eSignal. www.eSignal.com

229

Epilogue

So, here we are. We're at the end of *The ART® of Trading*. It seems like the journey was a quick one. Yet the reality is that the journey has just begun. The plan when we began Chapter 1 was to introduce you to reality-based trading and to a software tool called Applied Reality Trading—and, of course, to enable you to test-drive the ART software and enjoy the benefits of technical analysis in your trading and investing.

The hope is that, if you hadn't already done so before reading this book, you will now have become a number one fan of technical analysis—and ART. This means that you will be able to use these technical tools in a life-long journey of evaluating the markets that will enable you to take control over your financial destiny. All the while, you'll be exploring the financial markets at your own pace and with your own personal approach.

We encourage you to use Appendix D (Resources) at the back of the book to guide you toward a variety of recommended books, periodicals, data providers, brokers, and other vendors that may be helpful to you as a starting point. Be sure to do some research and call the companies listed to ask questions and find out which of these resources will be the right ones for your current needs.

Your comments and feedback are always welcome, and you can send me an e-mail via info@traderscoach.com. Drop me a line to let me know how you are progressing with the system. I want to thank you for sharing this journey with me and taking the time to explore the Applied Reality Trading system.

It is my sincere wish that the very most that you dream for be the least that you receive—in trading and in your life.

BENNETT A. MCDOWELL
San Diego, California
January 2008

About the DVD

INTRODUCTION

This appendix provides you with information on the contents of the DVD that accompanies this book. For the latest information, please refer to the ReadMe file located at the root of the DVD.

System Requirements

- Pentium processor-base PC or compatible computer running Windows XP Service Pack 2 or Vista, or 400 MHz Power PC G3 or faster Macintosh running Mac OS X v10.3.9, v10.4.9 or later
- At least 128 MB of total RAM installed on your computer; for best performance, we recommend at least 256 MB
- QuickTime or other player capable of viewing .mov file
- A DVD-ROM drive

USING THE DVD WITH WINDOWS

To install the items from the DVD to your hard drive, follow these steps:

1. Insert the DVD into your computer's DVD-ROM drive.
2. The DVD interface will appear. The interface provides a simple point-and-click way to explore the contents of the DVD.

If the opening screen of the DVD does not appear automatically, follow these steps to access the DVD:

1. Click the Start button on the left end of the taskbar and then choose Run from the menu that pops up.
2. In the dialog box that appears, type **d:\start.exe**. (If your DVD drive is not drive d, fill in the appropriate letter in place of *d*.) This brings up the DVD Interface described in the preceding set of steps.

WHAT'S ON THE DVD

The video provided places you in a classroom with Bennett McDowell, where he illustrates the concepts that have been presented throughout the pages of the book. What's more, the video brings the ART software to life showing how the color on your charts assist you in visually assessing the market.

Content

Instructional video. Bennett McDowell presents a tutorial of the concepts covered in the book and an introduction to the ART® trading program.

Color charts. The charts within the text appear in black and white, so the DVD will enable readers to see how the charts would look in color (as in the actual online trading program for ART).

Any material from the book, including forms, slides, and lesson plans, if available, are in the folder named "Content."

Applications

The following applications are on the DVD:

Adobe Reader   Adobe Reader is a freeware application for viewing files in the Adobe Portable Document format.

Shareware programs are fully functional, trial versions of copyrighted programs. If you like particular programs, register with their authors for a nominal fee and receive licenses, enhanced versions, and technical support.

Freeware programs are copyrighted games, applications, and utilities that are free for personal use. Unlike shareware, these programs do not require a fee or provide technical support.

GNU software is governed by its own license, which is included inside the folder of the GNU product. See the GNU license for more details.

Trial, demo, or evaluation versions are usually limited either by time or functionality (such as being unable to save projects). Some trial versions are very sensitive to system date changes. If you alter your computer's date, the programs will "time out" and no longer be functional.

Customer Care   If you have trouble with the DVD, please call the Wiley Product Technical Support phone number at 1-800-762-2974. Outside the United States, call 1-317-572-3994. You can also contact Wiley Product

Technical Support at **http://support.wiley.com**. John Wiley & Sons will provide technical support only for installation and other general quality control items. For technical support on the applications themselves, consult the program's vendor or author.

For technical support or customer service for other issues, please contact TradersCoach.com® by calling 1-800-695-6188. Outside the United States, call 1-858-695-0592. Or, e-mail us via support@traderscoach.com.

To place additional orders or to request information about other Wiley products, please call 1-877-762-2974.

ART Software Quick-Start

1. SELECT YOUR MARKET AND TIME FRAME

See Chapter 8 (Selecting a Financial Market) in this book to help you decide on which financial market you will start in, such as stocks, futures, options, forex, etc. Also see Chapter 9 (Selecting a Time Frame) and Chapter 6 (Identify Your Personal ART Profile) to determine what time frame suits your needs.

Regarding time frames, if you are investing, you may be able to work with longer time frames and will use end-of-day data. If you want to day trade, you will use shorter time frames, and will require real-time data.

Once you have determined what market and time frame you will start with, you will be able to decide on the ART platform that is compatible with your trading and investing needs.

2. SELECT YOUR ART PLATFORM, DATA FEED, AND BROKER

Go to Appendix D (Resources) at the back of this book, and review the available ART platforms that are compatible with the ART software. You may also go to www.TradersCoach.com to see if there have been any new ART platforms added since the time of this printing.

Your decision on which platform to select will depend on what market you would like to work in, the time frame you choose, which broker you plan to use, and which data feed you choose. (Or you may have an account open with one of the ART platforms already that is meeting your needs—which means you can skip to Quick-Start step 5.)

In Appendix D there is also a list of ART compatible brokers and data feeds. Keep in mind that some brokerage firms supply *free* live streaming data if you meet certain requirements, so you may obtain brokerage services and data from the same source.

Remember, not all brokers service all financial markets. For, example, if you plan to trade the forex market, not every broker will be able to place trades for you and provide forex data—foreign exchange is a specialized market. When researching, be sure to ask all broker and data feed vendors what markets they specialize in before choosing your ART platform. Then, select the platform that is going to support the market you will be working in.

3. OPEN AN ACCOUNT WITH YOUR ART PLATFORM

Contact the company that has the platform you will be plugging the ART software into. They will activate your account to the specifications you request. Remember, some of the platforms available are free, so you will want to ask questions to learn about what services each platform provides and what the costs are, if any. We have not listed service options or costs, since these will change over time. To get the most accurate current information, call the phone numbers provided in Appendix D (Resources) at the back of this book.

When you open your account, you will receive account information, passwords, and the like, that you will need when you register your ART software.

4. REGISTER YOUR ART SOFTWARE

Once you have your platform account open, go to www.TradersCoach.com to register your ART software. You will need certain information from this book and your new platform account information, so be sure to have these items handy while you are registering.

Your purchase of this book entitles you to a free 30-day trial of the ART software. Following your trial, you will be offered a very special price on either a lease or purchase option of ART so that you can continue to benefit from the ART system.

5. GET STARTED!

You are ready to start trading and investing with ART. Remember to paper-trade using the methods taught in this book, and when you have mastered the ART software, go into the market and use the science of technical analysis combined with the art of reality-based trading and investing to begin looking at your trading and finances in a whole new way.

Enjoy, and if you have any questions contact one of our service representatives via Team@TradersCoach.com.

ART Tips

1. Trade only with money you can afford to lose. Never trade with borrowed money.

2. Practice paper-trading until you are profitable before trading with real money. When paper-trading, use a trading account size that will be the same as you plan to use when trading with real money (e.g., if you plan to have a trading account of $10,000, make sure you paper-trade that size account).

3. Always set a stop-loss exit on every trade before entering any, and all, trades.

4. Always exit your trade when your stop-loss tells you to—don't second-guess your stop.

5. Never risk more than 2 percent of your trading account on any one trade.

$$\$ \text{Account Size} \times 2\% = \$ \text{Risk Amount}$$
$$\$25,000 \times 2\% = \$500$$

6. Use the proper trade size formula on every trade.

$$\frac{\$ \text{Risk Amount} - \text{Commission}}{\$ \text{Difference between Entry and Stop}} = \text{Trade Size in Shares or Contracts}$$

$$\frac{\$500 - \$80}{\$1.50} = 280 \, \text{Shares}$$

7. Never exceed an overall 6% risk (of your trading account size) at any given time.

8. In most cases, be sure your trading account size is not greater than 10 percent of your total net worth.

9. Take full responsibility for all of your trading results. Do not play the victim game and turn the markets into the enemy. Remember, the market is a safe place.

10. Maintain complete trading records. Determine average win, average loss, and percentage of wins versus percentage of losses. Analyze your trading records to determine profit versus loss. Evaluate areas to increase profit. (Use The Trader's Assistant record-keeping system by TradersCoach.com.)

11. Do your homework and believe you can be a winner. Profitability comes from confidence in your system and in yourself.

12. Take a "Private Tutorial" at TradersCoach.com to hone and improve your ART charting software skills while trading the markets live in real time.

DEVELOPING YOUR OWN TRADING SYSTEM

Only you can decide how you want to utilize the ART trading signals. You must develop the right method based on your own unique personality, beliefs about trading, and tolerance for risk. How aggressive do you want to be? Do you have the psychology to be a trend trader? Or do you prefer to scalp the markets with more active trading. Only you can answer these questions. There are no shortcuts—you must paper-trade and practice different combinations until you find the right mix for you. This is the hard work, but it also can be the fun work since you are developing your own trading system. Once customized and honed, this system can provide you with a lifetime of trading success. If done correctly, this development process can give you the confidence you will need to be successful in the markets.

ART Software Technical Support

INTRODUCTION

This book comes with a 30-day free trial of the ART software. The 30-day period does not begin and your ART software does not become activated until you register your software on the www.TradersCoach.com web site. Upon completing your 30-day trial, you are entitled to discounted rates on the ART software lease and ownership options.

Once you have registered your ART software (see Appendix A on how to register), your e-mail technical support will begin. It is important to understand that this 30-day ART trial is a very special free offer, which means that technical support will be limited to e-mail support only. There is a variety of additional support services available from www.TradersCoach.com for an additional fee if you require more assistance. Please call us at 858-695-0592 or visit the www.TradersCoach.com web site for more information.

Also, the e-mail technical support that you receive for 30 days is designed to troubleshoot technical issues only. For trading and investing methodology issues, refer to *The ART® of Trading* book, which, if studied, will answer your questions in detail.

HOW TO CONTACT US

Again, *technical support for the ART software is available via e-mail only.* We provide telephone support, but please understand that our telephone representatives are trained to answer general questions only and are not able to provide technical software support.

Technical E-mail Support

E-mail your detailed questions, 24 hours per day/7 days per week, to Support@TradersCoach.com.

Depending on the volume of e-mails we receive, your e-mail will be responded to in a time period from 1 hour to 24 hours from the receipt of your request. Support is given on a first-come, first-served basis. (Please understand that occasionally our technical support volume is huge—we appreciate your patience during these times.) To ensure the best possible technical response, please make sure your e-mails are detailed and clear.

General Telephone Support

Call us, 24 hours per day/7 days per week, at 1-858-695-0592.

WWW.TRADERSCOACH.COM

Log on to the TradersCoach.com web site and click on the color picture of the cover of this book, *The ART® of Trading*. There, you will also find a wealth of free technical and conceptual support services, including but not limited to the following:

- ART four-color charts in that you can view and print out.
- Videos you can download with step-by-step instructions on everything from how to load your software to how to use the ART signals.
- Page where you can register your ART software.

ART SOFTWARE EQUIPMENT REQUIREMENTS

To utilize your ART software trial that is included with this book, you will need to have the following equipment:

1. Power user requirements: Windows 2000; Windows XP; Windows Vista; 2.6 GHz Pentium 4 or compatible

2. Monitor with 1024 × 768 resolution; 512 MB RAM (*Note:* If you plan to work with multiple charts or have other programs open at the same time, you will need 1 GB RAM)

3. 60 MB available hard disk space

4. Internet connectivity: DSL; cable modem; ISDN; or T1 or T3

5. Microsoft Internet Explorer 6.0

6. Live data feed from the financial markets

Resources

ART PLATFORMS (COMPATIBLE WITH ART SOFTWARE AS OF JANUARY 2008)

TradeStation—ART Platform

www.TradeStation.com

Note: Ask about a very special free offer that you are entitled to with the purchase of this book, *The ART® of Trading.*

1-800-292-3476

1-954-652-7407

TradeStation is a premier and first-class broker, data provider, and ART platform. They provide a variety of services for virtually every trading and investing market. They are *not* compatible with other brokers or data vendors.

eSignal—ART Platform

www.eSignal.com

Contact: Ray Fitzgerald

Note: Ask about a very special free offer that you are entitled to with the purchase of this book, *The ART® of Trading.*

1-800-322-0940

1-510-723-1671

eSignal is a premier and first-class data provider and ART platform. They are *not* a broker, but they are compatible with many other brokers. Some of the brokers they are compatible with are TD Ameritrade, Interactive Brokers, IntesaTrade, Lind-Waldock, GAIN Capital, MB Trading, OptionsXpress, and TradeFreedom.

QuoteTracker—ART Platform

www.QuoteTracker.com

Contact: support@quotetracker.com

QuoteTracker is a premier and first-class trading and investing ART platform. They are *not* a broker and they are *not* a data provider. They are an interface between software platforms. They are compatible with TD Ameritrade brokerage services.

NinjaTrader—ART Platform

www.NinjaTrader.com

Contact: support@ninjatrader.com

NinjaTrader is a premier and first-class trading and investing ART platform. They are *not* a broker and they are *not* a data provider; they are an interface between software platforms. Some of the brokers they are compatible with are Interactive Brokers, Forex.com, MB Trading, AMP Futures & Forex, and Mirus Futures.com. Some of the data providers they are compatible with are eSignal, Open Tick, ZenFire, and DTN.IQ.

BROKERS (ORDER EXECUTION COMPATIBLE WITH ART SOFTWARE AS OF JANUARY 2008)

TD AmeriTrade—Broker

ART platform required: QuoteTracker or eSignal.

www.TDAmeriTrade.com

Note: Ask about a very special free offer that you are entitled to with the purchase of this book, *The ART® of Trading.*

1-800-454-9272

1-402-970-5805

TradeStation—Broker

ART platform required: TradeStation

www.TradeStation.com

Note: Ask about a very special free offer that you are entitled to with the purchase of this book, *The ART® of Trading.*

1-800-292-3476

1-954-652-7407

Interactive Brokers—Broker

ART platform required: eSignal or NinjaTrader

www.InteractiveBrokers.com

1-877-442-2757

1-312-542-6901

Lind-Waldock—Broker (Division of MAN Financial)

ART platform required: eSignal

www.lind-waldock.com

1-800-445-2000

1-312-788-2800

GAIN Capital—Broker

ART platform required: eSignal or NinjaTrader

www.GAINCapital.com

Forex.com—Broker

ART platform required: eSignal or NinjaTrader

www.Forex.com

MB Trading—Broker

ART platform required: eSignal or NinjaTrader

www.MBTrading.com

1-866-628-3001

1-310-647-4281

AMP Futures & Forex—Broker

ART platform required: NinjaTrader
www.ampfutures.com
1-800-560-1640
1-310-697-3242

Mirus Futures.com—Broker (Uses Zen-Fire Data)

ART platform required: NinjaTrader
www.MirusFutures.com
Contact: Eliot Wickersheimer
1-800-496-1683, ext. 2235
1-312-423-2235

OptionsXpress—Broker

ART platform required: eSignal
www.optionsxpress.com
1-888-280-6505
1-888-280-8020

Trade Freedom—Broker

ART platform required: eSignal
www.tradefreedom.com
Note: This is Canada's leading direct access broker.
1-866-837-3336
1-514-344-5111

FXCM—Broker

ART platform required: eSignal
www.fxcm.com
1-888-503-6739
1-212-897-7660

CMS Forex—Broker

ART platform required: eSignal
www.cmsforex.com

1-866-512-6739
1-212-563-2100

IntesaTrade—Broker

ART platform required: eSignal
www.intesatrade.it
Note: Specializes in international financial markets.

MF Global—Broker

ART platform required: NinjaTrader (Patsystems)
www.mfglobal.com

ND Global—Broker

ART platform required: NinjaTrader (Patsystems)
www.ndglobaltrading.com

Fox Futures—Broker

ART platform required: NinjaTrader (Patsystems)
www.foxfutures.com

RCG—Broker

ART platform required: NinjaTrader (Patsystems)
www.rcgdirect.com

Flash Futures—Broker

ART platform required: NinjaTrader (Patsystems)
www.flashfutures.com

Spike Trading—Broker

ART platform required: NinjaTrader (Patsystems)
www.spiketrading.com

DATA SOURCES (COMPATIBLE WITH ART SOFTWARE AS OF JANUARY 2008)

eSignal—Data

ART platform required: eSignal, QuoteTracker or NinjaTrader

www.eSignal.com

Contact: Ray Fitzgerald

Note: Ask about a very special free offer that you are entitled to with the purchase of this book, *The ART® of Trading.*

1-800-322-0940

1-510-723-1671

QuoteTracker—Data

ART platform required: QuoteTracker

www.QuoteTracker.com

Contact: support@quotetracker.com

TradeStation—Data

ART platform required: TradeStation

www.TradeStation.com

Note: Ask about a very special free offer that you are entitled to with the purchase of this book, *The ART® of Trading.*

1-800-292-3476

1-954-652-7407

IQFeed (DTN Markets)—Data

ART platform required: QuoteTracker, NinjaTrader, or TradeStation

www.iqfeed.net

Contact: Trent Smalley

Note: Ask about a very special free offer that you are entitled to with the purchase of this book, *The ART® of Trading.*

1-800-475-4755

1-800-511-0096 ext. 8435

1-402-255-8435

Open Tick—Data

ART platform required: NinjaTrader
www.OpenTick.com
888-673-6842
239-262-1628

Interactive Brokers—Data

ART platform required: eSignal or NinjaTrader
www.InteractiveBrokers.com
1-877-442-2757
1-312-542-6901

BOOK & VIDEO SOURCES

Amazon.com

www.Amazon.com

Traders Press

www.TradersPress.com
1-800-927-8222
1-864-298-0222

Traders Library

www.TradersLibrary.com
1-800-272-2855
1-410-964-0026

RECOMMENDED BOOKS AND AUTHORS

Douglas, Mark

Trading In The Zone: Master The Market With Confidence, Discipline And A Winning Attitude

New York Institute of Finance, 2000

Elliott, Ralph Nelson

Edited by: Robert Prechter, Jr.

R.N. Elliott's Masterworks: The Definitive Collection
New Classics Library, 1994

Hayden, John

The 21 Irrefutable Truths Of Trading
McGraw-Hill, 2000

Kiev, Ari

Trading To Win: The Psychology Of Mastering The Markets
John Wiley & Sons, 1998

McDowell, Bennett

A Trader's Money Management System
John Wiley & Sons, 2008

McMillan, Lawrence

McMillan On Options, 2nd Edition
John Wiley & Sons, 2004

Murphy, John

The Visual Investor: How to Spot Market Trends
John Wiley & Sons, 1996

Schwager, Jack

Market Wizards: Interviews With Top Traders
New York Institute of Finance, 1989

Williams, Bill

Trading Chaos, 2nd Edition
John Wiley & Sons, 2004

RECOMMENDED PERIODICALS

Technical Analysis of Stocks & Commodities Magazine

www.Traders.com

1-800-832-4642

1-206-938-0570

13 issues per year

$64.95 USD cost per year

Traders World Magazine

www.tradersworld.com

1-800-288-4266

1-417-882-9697

4 issues per year

$19.95 USD cost per year

Futures Magazine

www.futuresmag.com

1-800-458-1734

1-847-763-9252

11 issues per year

$68.00 USD cost per year

Active Trader Magazine

www.activetradermag.com

1-800-341-9384

1-312-775-5421

12 issues per year

$59.40 USD cost per year

SFO (Stocks, Futures, and Options) Magazine

www.sfomag.com

1-800-590-0919

1-319-268-0441

12 issues per year

IBD (*Investor's Business Daily*) Newspaper

www.investors.com

1-800-831-2525

1-310-448-6600

250 issues per year

$295.00 USD cost per year

The *Wall Street Journal* Newspaper

www.wsj.com

1-800-568-7625

360 issues per year

$249.00 USD cost per year

Barron's Newspaper

www.barronsmag.com

1-800-568-7625

45 issues per year

$179.00 USD cost per year

RECOMMENDED VIDEOS

Rogue Trader

Miramax, 2000

97 Minutes Running Time

Starring: Ewan McGregor

Director: James Deaden

This is a true story of Nick Leeson who is famous for causing the collapse of the Barings Bank in 1995. Barings was the oldest bank in the world (operating for 232 years before the collapse) and Leeson was a trader for the bank. The film does an amazing job of showing how an ordinary young man can allow small losses to spiral into huge $1 billion losses because of his own fear, greed, denial, and lack of risk control. It also shows how an established reputable bank could be so oblivious to let it happen. This is a remarkable tale that illustrates how emotions and psychology can get the better of anyone in the trading environment if one is not careful.

Wall Street

20th Century Fox, 1987

126 Minutes Running Time

Starring: Michael Douglas, Charlie Sheen, Daryl Hannah

Director: Oliver Stone

Pure Hollywood, this film is about an ambitious young broker (Charlie Sheen) who is lured into the illegal, lucrative world of corporate espionage when he is seduced by the power, status and financial wizardry of Wall Street legend Gordon Gekko (Michael Douglas). He soon discovers that the pursuit of overnight riches comes at a price that's too high to pay. Gordon Gekko's famous line in the movie is "... greed is good!" Very entertaining Wall Street fiction, this movie is fun to watch.

Boiler Room

New Line Films, 2000

120 Minutes Running Time

Starring: Giovanni Ribisi, Ben Affleck

Director: Ben Younger

This is a fictional story of Seth Davis (Giovanni Ribisi) who runs a small-time gambling casino operation out of his apartment. He is recruited by the city's newest and hottest stock brokerage firm, an aggressive, renegade firm far from the traditions of Wall Street. The firm has a huge team of high pressure telemarketing stock brokers who relentlessly call until they sell whatever the "stock du jour" for the firm is. Interesting and disturbing look at what can happen when unethical individuals gain the trust of unsuspecting investors.

RECOMMENDED EDUCATION

TradersCoach.com

Web site: www.TradersCoach.com

E-mail: team@traderscoach.com

Contact: Jean McDowell

Phone: 1-800-695-6188 or 1-858-695-0592

Founded in 1998 by Bennett A. McDowell, TradersCoach.com is a worldwide leader in trader education and support. Dedicated to providing a no-nonsense and honest approach to trading and investing in the financial markets, TradersCoach.com has impeccable integrity and is a member of the Better Business Bureau's online network.

The products and services offered include free monthly educational webcasts, the ART (Applied Reality Trading) technical analysis software, The Trader's Assistant record-keeping system, and the Trade Size Calculator software. In addition Bennett McDowell offers private coaching and consultations to traders around the world to give them the support they need. For extensive free trading information visit the web site listed above.

The Money Show University

Web site: www.moneyshow.com

Phone: 800-970-4355

A terrific educational source is MoneyShow.com University (see web site above). You'll find free courses that you can take online that come to you in the convenience of your own home or office. There are live streaming audio video classes presented by leaders in education, including Bennett A. McDowell. Be sure to take advantage of his course on Money Management, available to you free of charge.

The Learning Annex

Web site: www.learningannex.com

Phone: 212-371-0280

This innovative educational "school" was founded by Bill Zanker in 1980 in New York City. As you can see, the Learning Annex has grown and now has branches in a number of cities from coast to coast. We've provided you with the branches available to you at the time of this printing, but check the web site to see if there are additional locations opened since this book went to press.

For a nominal fee, you can attend live classes in a number of cities and have teachers such as Donald Trump, Deepak Chopra, and Bennett McDowell teach classes on trading, investing, real estate, and more.

The Learning Annex—San Diego, USA

Phone: 1-619-544-9700

The Learning Annex—San Francisco, USA
Phone: 1-415-788-5500

The Learning Annex—New York City, USA
Phone: 1-212-371-0280

The Learning Annex—Los Angeles, USA
Phone: 1-310-478-6677

The Learning Annex—Toronto, Canada
Phone: 1-416-964-0011

Trader's Expo Trade Shows

Web site: www.tradersexpo.com
Phone: 800-970-4355

The Trader's EXPO trade shows are geared towards the active trader and feature an extensive lineup of prominent speakers in the financial industry, including Bennett A. McDowell.

Attendance to most events is completely free of charge. The shows generally last two to four days, giving attendees ample time to participate in a variety of seminars and workshops on a broad range of trading topics from money management to system design.

The live trade shows are held in cities across the United States. For the latest information on schedule of cities and dates, please refer to the web site or call for more information (the phone number is shown below each listing). The information provided is current at the time of this printing; confirm current locations and dates as this information may become outdated.

Trader's EXPO—New York, USA
February of each year

Trader's EXPO—California, USA
Summer of each year

Trader's EXPO—Las Vegas, USA
November of each year

Forex Expo
November of each year

The Money Show Trade Shows

Web site: www.moneyshow.com/msc/investers/calendar.asp
Phone: 800-970-4355

The Money Show trade shows are geared towards the savvy investor and feature an extensive lineup of prominent speakers in the financial industry, including Bennett A. McDowell.

Attendance to most events is completely free of charge. The shows generally last two to four days, giving attendees ample time to participate in a variety of seminars and workshops on a broad range of trading topics from money management to retirement portfolio tips.

The trade shows are held in cities across the United States (with the exception of the Money Show in London, England). For the latest information on schedule of cities and dates, please refer to the Web site or phone number shown above. The information provided is current at the time of this printing; confirm current locations and dates as this information may become outdated.

The Money Show Tradeshow—San Francisco
August of each year

The Money Show Tradeshow—Washington DC
Autumn of each year

The Money Show Tradeshow—Las Vegas
May of each year

The World Money Show Tradeshow—London, England
December of each year

The World Money Show Tradeshow—Orlando, USA
February of each year

Colleagues In Trading

Web site: www.colleaguesintrading.com
Contact: Sharon Giriulat

This is a non-profit organization that provides valuable support and information to traders and investors. Their goal is to be equivalent to a "Good Housekeeping" seal of approval for firms in the financial and trading industry. They research and seek out trading products and services that meet their standards of excellence.

In addition, Colleagues In Trading has developed an approach they call the Trader's Life Cycle. This enables visitors to the web site to determine where in the Life Cycle they may currently be, and where they may want to move to. The web site has listings of seminars and lectures that are given by trading industry leaders, including Bennett A. McDowell.

TECHNOLOGY AND SOFTWARE

Worden

Web site: www.worden.com
E-mail: support@worden.com
Phone: 919-408-0542 or 800-776-4940

TeleChart has been the "Best Stock Software Under $200" for the past 12 years, as voted by the readers of *Stocks & Commodities* magazine. You can scan the entire NYSE, NASDAQ, and AMEX in seconds for stocks that fit your investing and trading style. Create your own integrated stock journal and rank stocks by almost any technical or fundamental condition you can think of.

Custom Trading Computers, Inc.

Web site: www.customtradingcomputers.com
E-mail: info@customtradingcomputers..com
Phone: 1-801-784-2294
Contact: Jordan Peterson

Custom Trading Computers is a leader in custom built trading computers that are designed specifically for trading the financial markets. They offer turnkey multiple monitor capable, performance-based computers, and ClearView multiscreen monitor arrays to maximize efficiency in your trading.

Glossary

Accumulation distribution (A/C): A momentum indicator that attempts to gauge supply and demand by determining whether traders or investors are "accumulating" (buying) or "distributing" (selling) a certain financial instrument by identifying divergences between price and volume flow.

American Stock Exchange (AMEX): The second largest stock exchange in the United States after the NYSE. Generally the listing rules are more lenient than those of the NYSE, and therefore the AMEX has a larger representation of stocks and bonds issued by smaller companies.

Applied Reality Trading (ART): Applied Reality Trading is a technical analysis system developed by Bennett A. McDowell that focuses on trading the realities of the financial markets. The ART software works on any time frame and in any market for both investors and day traders. The software generates charts that illustrate clear entry and exit signals and sound money management rules.

ART bear price bar: When prices close on the lower half of the bar, it is an ART bear price bar. The bar is defined by the relation between the close and the price bar interval. The bears are in control at the close of the price bar. (ART determines bear and bull differently than other systems.)

ART bull price bar: When prices close on the upper half of the bar, it is an ART bull price bar. The bar is defined by the relation between the CLOSE and the price bar interval. The bulls are in control at the close of the price bar. (ART determines bear and bull differently than other systems.)

ART elongated price bar: This price bar is at least one-third longer than the previous three to five price bars.

ART inside price bar: A compressed price bar forming directly after the signal bar in an ART Reversal. It can be used to aggressively enter an ART Reversal trade.

ART neutral price bar: On this price bar, the open and the close are at the 50 percent point on the bar when it closes. Both bulls and bears are in stalemate at the close of the price bar.

ART One-Bar Reversal (1B): This scalp signal identifies exact entries and exits. It can also be used for scaling in and scaling out of trends. This reversal signal requires only one price bar that is the signal bar, which determines both the entry and also the stop-loss exit. It can be used on all markets and all time frames.

ART signal price bar: Represents the price bar used for a trade entry when using the ART reversals. The ART trading software designates the ART signal bar with a 1B or 2B directly above or below the price bar.

ART Two-Bar Reversal (2B): This scalp signal identifies exact entries and exits. It can also be used for scaling in and scaling out of trends. This reversal signal requires two price bars, the first price bar is used for the stop-loss exit and the second price bar or signal bar is used for the entry. It can be used on all markets and all time frames.

Ask price: Also known as the offer. The price a seller is willing to accept. The difference between the bid and ask is known as the bid–ask spread.

Asset allocation: The process of deciding what types of assets you want to own, and the percentage of each. As conditions change, the percent allotted to each asset class changes.

Average true range (ATR): Helps determine a market's volatility over a given period. It is calculated by taking an average of the true ranges over a set number of previous periods. It is the (moving) average of the true range for a given period.

Balance sheet: A listing of all assets and liabilities for an individual or a business. The surplus of assets over liabilities is the net worth, or what is owned free of debt.

Bear: Someone who believes prices will decline and is generally pessimistic about future market returns.

Bear market: A market characterized by prolonged broad declining prices. Some negative information has entered the market to create this condition. Generally the downturn in price is in excess of 20 percent. Not to be confused with a correction.

Bid–ask spread: The difference between the bid and the ask. The spread narrows or widens according to the supply and demand for the security being traded.

Bid price: The price a buyer is willing to pay.

"Black box" system: This is a 100 percent mechanical system that requires absolutely *no* discretion. The concern with these systems is that they are unable to adapt to ever-changing market cycles. The reality is that over time all systems require some form of discretionary decision making to be consistently profitable. ART is not a black box system.

Blue chip: A large, nationally recognized, financially sound firm with a long track record usually selling high-quality and widely accepted goods and services. *Examples:* General Electric and IBM.

Bond: A debt investment. Investors lend money to an institution by buying bonds and receive fixed interest payments in return. When the bond matures, the investor receives the principal back.

Bond market: The bond market, also known as the debt, credit, or fixed-income market, is a financial market where participants buy and sell debt securities usually in the form of bonds.

Bracketed market: This is also known as a consolidating, channeled, sideways, or nontrending market. When a market is bracketed it is stuck in a price range between an identifiable "resistance" and "support" level. On a chart, a bracket will be seen as a horizontal line. Some of the most powerful and profitable trends come out of markets that have been bracketed for more than 20 price bars.

Breakout: A sharp change in price movement after the market has traded sideways for at least 20 price bars. This is beyond a previous high (or low) or outside the boundaries of a preceding price bracket or consolidation.

Bull: Someone who believes that prices will rise and is generally optimistic about future market returns.

Bull market: A market characterized by prolonged broad rising prices. Positive information has entered the market to create this condition. Over 70 percent of historic periods have been bull markets.

Call: An options contract with the right to buy a specific number of shares of a stock at a specified price (the strike price) on or before a specific expiration date, regardless of the underlying stock's current market price. A call option writer sells the right to a buyer.

Candlesticks: A type of bar chart developed by the Japanese, in which the price range between the open and the close is either a white rectangle (if the close is higher) or a black rectangle (if the close is lower).

Capital: The money you need to trade or invest. This should be "risk" capital, meaning that you can afford to lose this money.

Cash per share: The amount of cash divided by the total number of common stock shares outstanding for a given stock. A corporation with high cash per share ratio is said to be cash rich and may be considered low risk or undervalued.

Central bank: The institution in each country responsible for setting monetary policy, print money, managing reserves, and controlling inflation. In the United States, the central bank is the Federal Reserve System, also known as the Fed.

Channeling market: This is also known as a bracketed, consolidating, sideways or nontrending market. See *Bracketed market.*

Chart: A graph that depicts the price movement of a given market. The most common type of chart is the bar chart, which denotes each interval's open, high, low, and close for a given market with a single price bar.

Chart analysis: The study of price charts in an effort to find patterns that in the past preceded price advances or declines. The basic concept is that the development of similar patterns in a current market can signal a probable market move in the same direction. Practitioners of chart analysis are often referred to as "technical analysis" traders or investors.

Chicago Board of Trade (CBOT):   Established in 1848, as a leading futures and options on futures exchange. More than 3,600 CBOT members trade 50 different futures and options products at the exchange through open auction and/or electronically. CME Group is a combined entity formed by the 2007 merger of the Chicago Mercantile Exchange (CME) and the Chicago Board of Trade (CBOT).

Chicago Board Options Exchange (CBOE):   Founded in 1973, the CBOE is an exchange that focuses on options contracts for individual equities, indexes and interest rates. The CBOE is the world's largest options market. It captures a majority of the options traded. It is also a market leader in developing new financial products and technological innovation, particularly with electronic trading.

Chicago Mercantile Exchange (CME):   Founded in 1898 as the Chicago Butter and Egg Board, this is an American financial exchange based in Chicago. Originally. the exchange was a not-for-profit organization. The exchange demutualized in November 2000, went public in December 2002, and merged with the Chicago Board of Trade in July 2007. CME trades several types of financial instruments: interest rates, equities, currencies, and commodities. CME has the largest options and futures contracts open interest (number of contracts outstanding) of any future exchange in the world. Trading is conducted in two methods; an open outcry format and the CME Globex® electronic trading platform. Approximately 70 percent of total volume at the exchange occurs on CME Globex.

Chicago Mercantile Group (CME Group):   The world's largest and most diverse exchange. Formed by the 2007 merger of the Chicago Mercantile Exchange (CME) and the Chicago Board of Trade (CBOT), CME Group serves the risk management needs of customers around the globe. As an international marketplace, CME Group brings buyers and sellers together on the CME Globex electronic trading platform and on its trading floors.

Churning (excessive trading):   When a broker excessively trades an account for the purpose of increasing his or her commission revenue it is referred to as "churning." This practice is entirely unethical and does not serve the customer's investment or trading goals.

Commission: Fees paid to a brokerage house to execute a transaction.

Commodities: Physical goods that are traded at a futures exchange such as grains, foods, meats, metals, etc.

Consolidating market: This is also known as a bracketed, channeled, sideways or nontrending market. See *Bracketed market.*

Consumer Price Index (CPI): Issued by the Bureau of Labor Statistics, this figure is a popularly used measure of inflation. It measures the relative change in prices of a basket of consumer products and services.

Contract: A single unit of a commodity or future. This is similar to shares in stocks.

Contrarian: One who trades or invests on contrary opinion using the theory that they can profit by doing the opposite of the majority of traders or investors in the market.

Correction: A short, sharp reverse in prices during a longer market trend.

Corrective Elliott Wave: Refers to an Elliott Wave structure made up of impulsive wave counts and corrective wave counts. Usually refers to a correction wave sequence in an impulsive trend wave sequence.

Countertrend trade: A trading strategy where an investor or trader attempts to make small gains through a series of trades against the current trend.

Cover: To liquidate an existing position (such as sell if one is long; buy if one is short).

Covered call: To sell a call option. At the same time you own the same number of shares represented by the option in the underlying stock.

Covered put: To sell a put option. At the same time you are holding a short position in the underlying stock.

Data: Live streaming market data is provided to the trader or investor by data providers and brokerage houses. This data is used to conduct technical analysis and provides price and volume information. "Real-time" data is sent by the minute during the trading day. Generally, data providers charge more for real-time data because it is more labor intensive to provide. Real-time data is used by day-traders. End-of-day data is provided at the end of the day and gives you final price and volume information for the market you are analyzing. Data providers charge less for end-of-day data and this type of data is used more by investors and position traders.

Day trade: A trade that is liquidated on the same day it is initiated.

Day trader: Day trading refers to the practice of buying and selling financial instruments within the same trading day such that all positions will usually (not necessarily always) be closed before the market close. Traders who participate in day trading are day traders.

Debt-to-equity ratio: Ratio demonstrating an institution's debt relative to its equity. Just one component used by corporations in assessing optimal capital structures.

Decimals: Increment of movement in the stock market.

Deflation: A drop in average product and services price levels, usually caused by excessive tightening of money supply. Deflation can lead to reduced economic demand and higher unemployment. Not to be confused with disinflation.

Discretionary trader: A trader who makes decisions based on his own analysis of the market, rather than in response to signals generated by a computerized "black box" system. The best discretionary traders are those who develop a systematic approach and then use discretion in their entries, exits, and position sizing to improve performance.

Disinflation: The slowing growth of average product and services price levels. This can be thought of as the slowing of inflation. Not to be confused with deflation.

Divergence: The failure of a market or indicator to follow suit when a related market or indicator sets a new high or low. Some analysts look for divergences as a signal of impending market tops and bottoms.

Diversification: Trading or investing in a variety of markets and sectors to reduce risk. Don't put all your eggs in one basket!

Dividend: A payment made to stock holders, usually quarterly, out of a firm's current or retained earnings.

Dollar cost averaging: Averaging the cost per share of a particular security by investing a fixed sum regularly.

Double witching: A term used for the day when both options and futures expire.

Doubling down: Adding on to a losing position is considered doubling down.

Dow Jones Industrial Average (DJIA): A price-weighted index of 30 blue-chip U.S. stocks. This index is also known as the "Dow."

Downtrend: A general tendency for declining prices in a given market.

Drawdown: A decrease in the value of your account because of losing trades or because of "paper losses" which may occur simply because of a decline in value of open positions. Low drawdown is a desirable performance feature of a trader or investor.

E-mini: Used in the futures market to represent a smaller trading market of its parent market.

Earnings per share (EPS): A firm's total after-tax net earnings divided by the number of common shares outstanding.

Earnings-to-price ratio (E/P): Ratio of a company's earnings per share to its share price. This is the reverse of the price to earnings ratio.

Efficient market: The theory that the financial markets quickly and efficiently compensate and price-in all widely known information.

Electronic communication network (ECN): ARCA, ATTN, BTRD, ISLD, REDI, and STRK are examples of ECNs.

Elliott Wave analysis: A method of market analysis based on the theories of Ralph Nelson Elliott. Although relatively complex, the basic theory is based on the concept that markets move in waves, forming a general pattern of five waves (or market legs) in the direction of the main trend, followed by three corrective waves in the opposite direction.

Entry: The point at which you place or open your trade or investment. This is the opposite of your exit. When placing your entry, you should already know what your initial exit will be—this is called your stop-loss exit. The distance between your entry and your exit will determine what your trade size will be.

Equities markets: Stock markets.

Equity: The total dollar value of an account.

Equity curve: The value of your account over time, illustrated in a graph.

Exchange-traded fund (ETF): A security that tracks a specific index, equity category, or other basket of assets but is traded on an exchange like a single stock.

Exercise an option: To buy or sell a call or put option by the expiration date on the options contract.

Exit: The point at which you close your trade or investment. This is the opposite of your entry. It can also be known as your stop-loss exit. It is a crucial part of your money management risk control plan. The distance between your entry and your exit will determine what your trade size will be.

False breakout: A short-lived price move that penetrates a prior high or low before succumbing to a pronounced price move in the opposite direction. For example, if the price of a stock that has traded between $18 and $20 then rises to $21 and then quickly falls below $18, the move to $21 can be termed a false breakout.

Federal Open Market Committee (FOMC): A 12-member committee responsible for setting credit and interest rate policy for the Federal Reserve System. They set the discount rate directly and control the federal funds rate by buying and selling government securities impacting the rate. They meet eight times a year under the direction of a chairman.

Federal Reserve Board of Governors: The governing arm of the Federal Reserve System, which seeks to regulate the economy through the implementation of monetary policy. The seven members of the Board of Governors are appointed by United States presidents to serve 14-year terms.

Federal Reserve System (Fed): The United States central banking system, responsible for regulating the flow of money and credit. It serves as a bank for other banks and the United States government.

Fibonacci retracements: The concept that retracements of prior trends will often approximate 38.2 percent and 61.8 percent—numbers derived from the Fibonacci sequence.

Fibonacci sequence: A sequence of numbers that begins with 1,1 and progresses to infinity, with each number in the sequence equal to the sum of the preceding two numbers. Thus, the initial numbers in the sequence would be 1, 1, 2, 3, 5, 8, 13, 21, 34, 55, 89, etc. The ratio of consecutive numbers in the sequence converges to 0.618 as the numbers get larger. The ratio of alternate numbers in the sequence (for example, 21 and 55) converges to 0.382 as the numbers get larger. These two ratios—0.618 and 0.382—are commonly used to project retracements of prior price swings.

Fill: The price at which an order is executed is considered a fill. For example, if a trade were placed at $32.00 and filled at $32.25, the fill price would be $32.25.

Filter: An indicator that selects only data which meet specific criteria. Too many filters can lead to overoptimization.

Financial instruments: A term used to denote any form of funding medium. They can be categorized by whether they are cash instruments or derivative instruments. Cash instruments are financial instruments whose value is determined directly by markets. They can be divided into securities, which are readily transferable, and other cash instruments such as loans and deposits, where both borrower and lender have to agree on a transfer. Derivative instruments are financial instruments that derive their value from some other financial instrument or variable. They can be divided into exchange-traded derivatives and over-the-counter (OTC) derivatives. If it is debt, it can be further categorized into short term (less than one year) or long term. Foreign exchange instruments and transactions are neither debt nor equity based and belong in their own category.

Flat: When you are not in the market with a live position or when you close out all your positions before end of the trading day you are considered flat.

Floor trader: A member of the exchange who trades on the floor for personal profit.

Forecasts: Individuals that attempt to predict future market behavior are said to be "forecasting" the market. They tend to use indicators such as MACD, stochastics, and Elliott Waves to determine their forecasts. Forecasting the markets is often like forecasting the weather; it is difficult to do with any consistent accuracy.

Forex market: The foreign exchange market exists wherever one currency is traded for another. It is by far the largest financial market in the world, and includes trading between large banks, central banks, currency speculators, multinational corporations, governments, and other financial markets and institutions.

Fundamental analysis: The use of economic data and news data to analyze financial markets. For example, fundamental analysis of a currency might focus on such items as relative inflation rates, interest rates, economic growth rates, and political factors. In evaluating a stock a fundamental analyst would look at financials, value, earnings, debt, management, operations, competition and other relative data. Fundamental analysis is often contrasted with technical analysis, and some investors and traders use a combination of the two.

Futures: When commodity exchanges added stock index contracts and currency contracts, the term *futures* was developed to be more inclusive.

Futures market: An auction market in which participants buy and sell commodity/futures contracts for delivery on a specified future date. Trading is carried on through open yelling and hand signals in a trading pit.

Gann analysis: Market analysis based on a variety of technical concepts developed by William Gann, a famous stock and commodity trader during the first half of the twentieth century.

Gap: A price zone at which no trades occur. For example, if a market that has previously traded at a high of $20 opens at $22 on the following day. The price zone between $20 and $22 is referred to as a gap-up.

GLOBEX®:   Today the CME Globex trading system operates at the heart of CME. Proposed in 1987, it was introduced in 1992 as the first global electronic trading platform for futures contracts. This fully electronic trading system allows market participants to trade from booths at the exchange or while sitting in a home or office thousands of miles away.

Good 'til canceled (GTC):   By choosing GTC your order will remain open until it is executed or canceled, regardless of the number of trading days.

Gross domestic product (GDP):   The monetary value of all products and services produced in a country over a certain time period. In the United States, the GDP's growth is a popularly used indicator of overall economic health.

Grounded assessments: Trading and investing rules that are based on reality versus forecasts or predictions. For example, trade and investment entries based on price and volume would be considered "grounded assessments." The ART signals are all grounded assessments.

Hedge: To reduce risk in an investment or trade by offsetting it with another investment or trade.

Hedge fund: A managed portfolio of investments that is generally unregulated (unlike a mutual fund) and may invest in any highly speculative markets, including options.

Hedger: A market participant who implements a position to reduce price risk. The hedger's risk position is exactly opposite that of the speculator, who accepts risk in implementing positions to profit from anticipated price moves.

High probability: Trades or investments that statistically have a higher probability for success.

Higher-time-frame filter: A filter technique used to look at the market you are trading or investing in on a higher time frame to see if it confirms your primary time frame.

Hyperbolic move: A sharp and significant move to the up- or downside of your position. You might decide to scale out of a position to lock in profit if this type of move occurs.

Immediate or cancel (IOC):   By choosing IOC, your order will have immediate execution of all or part of the quantity of stock you specified. Any portion of the order that is not executed immediately is automatically canceled.

Impulsive Elliott Wave: The major trend in every time frame takes the form of five waves (impulse waves) which, once complete, are corrected by three waves (corrective waves).

Index Fund: A mutual fund that tracks a stated market index.

Individual retirement account (IRA):   A retirement account any employed person (or spouse of an employed person) can open and contribute to. Assets in the account grow tax deferred and contributions may be tax deductible. Distributions taken before age 59 are subject to penalty.

Inflation: Rate of increase in average product and service price levels. Different indexes use different baskets of products and services to compute the average prices. A popular index is the Consumer Price Index.

Initial public offering (IPO):   The first sale of equities (stocks) to the public by a private firm. In making an IPO, a private firm has "gone public."

Institutional investor: A bank, mutual fund, pension fund, or other corporate entity that trades financial instruments in large volumes.

Intraday time frame: A shorter time frame from the 1-minute to the 60-minute that day traders use in making their entry and exit decisions.

Investing: This is a term with several closely-related meanings in business management, finance and economics, related to saving or deferring consumption. An asset is usually purchased, or equivalently a deposit is made in a bank, in hopes of getting a future return or interest from it. Literally, the word means the "action of putting something in to somewhere else." Think of it as using financial instruments to invest savings for future gain and usually is not considered a short-term endeavor.

Investor: Generally uses a buy-and-hold approach using weekly and monthly charts to evaluate the market. An investor can be a trader when they time their long-term investments. They are more likely to incorporate fundamental analysis into their approach than a day trader would.

In-the-money: When an option's current market price is above the strike price of a call, or below the strike price of a put. An in-the-money option would produce a profit, if exercised.

Large cap: Refers to the size of a firm's market capitalization. Generally, any firms with a market cap above $10 billion are referred to as a large cap.

Left brain: The human brain is divided into two hemispheres, the left and the right, each of which is responsible for specific functions in human behavior and existence. The left brain is responsible primarily for speech, logic, planning, and analysis abilities. It tends to think in words as opposed to pictures and looks at the details as opposed to the big picture. Those of us that are analytical and scientific in nature are generally referred to as "left brain thinkers."

Leverage: The ability to control a dollar amount of a commodity or financial instrument greater than the amount of personal capital employed. This ability is obtained by using borrowed money, such as a margin account. The greater the leverage of the position, the greater the potential is for profit or loss.

Limit order: This is an order in which you can set the maximum price you want to pay for your purchase, or a minimum price you will accept as a seller.

Limit position: For many futures contracts, government regulations specify a maximum position size (such as number of contracts) that a speculator may hold.

Limit price move: For many futures contracts, the exchanges specify a maximum amount by which the price can change on a single day. A market that increases in price by this specified maximum is said to be limit-up, while a market that declines by the maximum is said to be limit-down.

Liquid market: A market in which there is a large number of trades daily so that most buy and sell orders can be executed without dramatically moving prices. In other words, a liquid market allows you the ease of entry and exit.

Liquidity: The degree to which a given market is liquid. When volume is high, there is usually a lot of liquidity. Low liquidity in markets can result in poor fills.

Long: A position established with a buy order, which profits in a rising price market. The term is also used to refer to the person or entity holding such a position.

Long call: To buy a call option.

Long put: To buy a put option.

Lot: The quantity of shares in which stocks are bought or sold. In futures markets, a lot is called a contract.

Margin: To borrow money from a financial provider (broker or bank) to purchase certain financial instruments.

Margin call: A Federal Reserve Board and financial service provider requirement that you deposit additional funds or sell some of your holdings to increase the equity in your margin account if it has fallen below the minimum.

Margin debit: The amount of money borrowed from a financial service provider.

Market index: This is the weighted average of companies comprising an index. The index represents a category or market (such as the S&P 500 or the Nasdaq).

Market maker: A broker, bank, or firm such as Goldman Sachs or Merrill Lynch, which buys or sells a security, currency, or futures contract.

Market order: Order to execute a purchase or sale for the best price available at the time the order is received.

Market risk: Uncontrolled risk possibilities that are always present in open trade and investment positions are considered market risk. Economic and world events can cause market risk where the market could move so quickly that you may not be able to exit at your stop-loss exit point.

Minneapolis Grain Exchange (MGEX):   This exchange was founded as a not-for-profit membership organization and maintains that structure today with a membership base of 390 outstanding seats, or memberships. In 1883, MGEX launched its first futures contract, hard red spring wheat, which is the exchange's most heavily traded product today.

Minor Pyramid Trading Point (MP):   An MP indicates a correction in the dominant trend.

Momentum investing and trading: Momentum represents the change in price now from some fixed time period in the past. This strategy attempts to capture short-term price movements based on the belief that price patterns are indicative of future results.

Money flow index (MFI):   A volume-weighted momentum indicator that measures the strength of money flowing in and out of a financial instrument. It compares "positive money flow" to "negative money flow" to create an indicator that can be compared to price in order to identify the strength or weakness of a trend. The MFI is measured on a 0 to 100 scale and is often calculated using a 14-day period.

Money management: The use of various methods of risk control in trading and investing. These methods include: (1) using proper trade size; (2) not risking more than 2 percent of your risk account on any one trade; and (3) diversifying your trading or investing account over a number of markets and sectors. This is also known as risk management.

Moving average (MA):   An average of data for a certain number of time periods. It "moves" because for each calculation, we use the latest number of time periods' data. By definition, a moving average lags the market. An exponentially smoothed moving average (EMA) gives greater weight to the more recent data, in an attempt to reduce the lag time.

Moving average convergence/divergence (MACD):   This is an indicator developed by Gerald Appel. It is calculated by subtracting the 26-period exponential moving average of a given financial instrument from its 12-period exponential moving average. By comparing moving averages, MACD displays trend following characteristics, and by plotting the difference of the moving averages as an oscillator, MACD displays momentum characteristics. The MACD histogram is the visual representation of the difference between the MACD line and the MACD signal line.

Mutual fund: An investment company investing in a variety of securities as dictated by the specific fund's prospectus. Investors do not own the underlying investments; they buy shares of the fund itself.

Naked option: A short option position by a trader who does not own the underlying commodity or financial instrument.

Naked put: A put option in which the seller does not own the short position. Loss potential is total except for the premium.

Nasdaq 100 Index: A modified capitalization-weighted index designed to track the performance of the 100 largest and most actively traded nonfinancial domestic and international securities listed on the Nasdaq Stock Market.

National Association of Securities Dealers Automated Quotations System (Nasdaq): The Nasdaq is an American stock market. It was founded in 1971 by the NASD, who divested themselves of it in a series of sales in 2000 and 2001. It is owned and operated by the Nasdaq Stock Market, Inc. the stock of which was listed on its own stock exchange in 2002. NASDAQ is the largest electronic screen-based equity securities market in the United States. With approximately 3,200 companies, it lists more companies and on average trades more shares per day than any other U.S. market.

National Association of Securities Dealers, Inc. (NASD): This self-regulatory organization of the securities industry is responsible for the regulation of the Nasdaq Stock Market and the over the counter markets.

Net asset value (NAV): This is an increment of movement in the mutual fund market.

Net worth: Total assets minus total liabilities equals net worth.

New York Cotton Exchange (NYCE): Was founded in 1870 by a group of one hundred cotton brokers and merchants in New York City. The oldest commodities exchange in the city, well into the twentieth century, cotton was a leading American commodity for both export and domestic consumption.

New York Futures Exchange (NYFE): An exchange on which trading occurs for Treasury Bond futures and some currency futures.

New York Mercantile Exchange (NYMEX): This is the world's largest physical commodity futures exchange, located in New York City. Its two principal divisions are the NYMEX and the New York Commodities Exchange (COMEX), which were once independent companies but are now merged.

New York Stock Exchange (NYSE): Known as the "Big Board," this is a New York City–based stock exchange. The NYSE provides an efficient method for buyers and sellers to trade shares of stock in companies registered for public trading. The exchange provides efficient price discovery via an auction environment designed to produce the fairest price for both parties. As of January 24, 2007, all NYSE stocks can be traded via its electronic hybrid market (except for a small group of very high-priced stocks). Customers can now send orders for immediate electronic execution or route orders to the floor for trade in the auction market. In excess of 50 percent of all order flow is now delivered to the floor electronically.

Nontrending market: This is also known as a bracketed, consolidating, channeled or sideways market. See *Bracketed market*.

NYSE Composite Index: A capitalization-weighted index designed to track the performance of all common stocks listed on the New York Stock Exchange.

On-balance volume (OBV): This method is used in technical analysis to detect momentum, the calculation of which relates volume to price change. OBV provides a running total of volume and shows whether this volume is flowing in or out of a given financial instrument. It attempts to detect when a stock, bond, etc. is being accumulated by a large number of buyers or sold by many sellers. This indicator was developed by Joe Granville.

Open interest: In futures markets, the total number of open and short positions are always equal. This total (long or short) is called the open interest. By definition, when a contract month first begins trading, the open interest is zero. The open interest then builds to a peak and declines as positions are liquidated approaching its expiration date.

Open order: An order to buy or sell a security that remains in effect until it is either canceled by the customer or executed.

Opening (OPG): At the opening, by choosing OPG, your order will be executed at the opening price. If it is not executed at the opening, it will be canceled automatically.

Optimization: This refers to optimizing software and the process of discovering what impact is the result of varying a particular parameter across different values; then using that information to make an informed decision about which specific parameter values to use in actual trading or investing.

Options: The right to buy or sell an underlying asset at a fixed price up to some specified date in the future. The right to buy is a call option, and the right to sell is a put option.

Options market: An open market to trade options.

Oscillator: Most oscillators go from 0 to 100. Analysts believe that when the indicator is near zero, the price is "oversold," and that when the price is near 100 it is "overbought."

Overtrading: You can tell when you are overtrading when your commission fees are eating into your profit or when you feel out of control. Stop and reverse (SAR) traders can overtrade because of the speed of their entries and exits.

Overbought/oversold indicator: An indicator that attempts to define when prices have risen (or fallen) too far, too fast, and hence are vulnerable to a reaction in the opposite direction.

Out-of-the-money: When an option's current market price is below the strike price of a call or above the strike price of a put.

Pacific Stock Exchange (PCX):   This was a regional stock exchange located in San Francisco, California. Its history begins with the founding of the San Francisco Stock and Bond exchange in 1882. Seven years later, the Los Angeles Oil Exchange was founded. In 1957, the two exchanges merged to form the Pacific Coast Stock Exchange, though trading floors were kept in both original cities. A name change to the Pacific Stock Exchange took place in 1973. Options trading began three years later. In 1997, "Stock" was dropped from the exchange's name. In 1999, the Pacific Exchange was the first United States stock exchange to demutualize. In 2001, the Los Angeles trading floor was closed, and the next year the San Francisco trading floor was closed as well. Pacific Exchange equities trading now takes place exclusively through NYSE Arca (formerly known as ArcaEx), an Electronic Communications Network. In 2003, the Pacific Exchange launched PCX plus, an electronic options trading platform.

Pattern recognition: A price-forecasting method that uses historical chart patterns to draw analogies to current situations.

Payoff ratio: Average winning trade divided by average losing trade equals payoff ratio (example: two wins to one loss payoff ratio).

Percentage in point (PIP):   The increment of movement in the forex market.

Pit: The area where a futures contract is traded on the exchange floor.

Position: Your financial stake in a given financial instrument or market.

Position trader: Uses daily and weekly charts to base their decisions and holds positions for days, weeks or months.

Price: In trading and investing, "price" refers to the last trade price.

Price bar: The price bar represents the high and low price behavior in a measured time interval. Price bars can represent different time frames (intervals) such as 1-minute, 5-minute, daily, weekly, etc.

Price oscillator (PPO) histogram: An indicator based on the difference between two moving averages and expressed as either a percentage or in absolute terms. The plot is presented as a histogram so that centerline crossovers and divergences are easily identifiable. The same principles apply to the MACD histogram.

Price-to-earnings (P/E) ratio: The current price of a stock divided by the company's annual earnings. One of the most commonly used stock valuation ratios.

Psychology: Mastering the psychology of trading and investing is a crucial part of becoming successful. The *trader's mind-set* is our definition of what you will attain when you have mastered your financial psychology. Some of the challenges in developing strong psychology are overcoming fear, greed, ego and anger when trading and investing.

PTP apex: The apex always points in the direction of the trend and is the point of the pyramid (triangle). It will tell you where to enter based on current market dynamics.

PTP base leg: The base leg is the flat base of the pyramid (triangle) and tells you where you will set your stop-loss exit based on current market dynamics.

PTP confirmed: When the market moves beyond the PTP apex in the direction of the trend, it will be confirmed. At that moment the triangle will turn either green or red, depending on whether it is a bull or bear trend.

PTP MinScore: This adjustable setting on the ART software determines the number of pyramids you will see on your chart.

PTP potential: When the pyramid is potential, it will be yellow in color. Once the market moves beyond the apex of the pyramid, it will then be confirmed and will turn either green or red depending on whether it is a bull or bear trend. If the market does not confirm the pyramid by exceeding the apex, the yellow pyramid (triangle) will disappear.

PTP voided: If a potential yellow pyramid is not confirmed, it will be voided and will disappear.

Put: An options contract with the right to sell a security at a specified exercise price on or before a specific expiration date.

Put option: This is the right to sell a stock (or bond or commodity) at a certain price by a certain date. A put option writer sells the right to a buyer. If the option exercises, the buyer "puts" the stock to the writer, and the writer must buy it.

Primary Pyramid Trading Point (P):   This ART signal indicates entries and exits into a primary trend trade or investment.

Pyramid Trading Point (PTP):   This ART trend trading signal was developed by Bennett A. McDowell and identifies exact entries and exits. It enables you to trade and invest utilizing the "realities" of the markets. It can be used on all markets and all time frames.

Reality-based trading: Living in reality is to be seeing and reacting to changes in the environment as they are occurring without attempting to predict future events. When one is living in reality they are dealing with what is actually occurring to them at any given moment. When one is trading and investing in reality, they are focusing on the current moment. They are void of opinions and other past or future distractions or thoughts. Reality-based trading and investing involves looking at what is "real" in the market such as price and volume.

Recession: A contraction in the business cycle, usually manifesting in slow or negative GDP growth.

Relative strength indicator (RSI):   An indicator developed by J. Wells Wilder, Jr., that is used to ascertain overbought and oversold conditions. It works on a scale of 99 to 1 with 99 being the strongest and 1 being the weakest. In the stock market, a measure of a given stock's price strength relative to a broad index of stocks. The term can also be used in a more general sense to refer to an overbought/oversold type of indicator.

Resistance: In technical analysis, a price area at which a rising market is expected to encounter increased selling pressure sufficient to stall or reverse the advance.

Retracement: A price movement in the opposite direction of the previous trend. A retracement is usually a price correction. For example, in a rising market, a 55 percent retracement would indicate a price decline equal to 55 percent of the prior advance.

Reward-to-risk ratio: The average winning trade divided by the size of the average losing trade. This formula will enable you to determine the estimated potential loss or gain of future transactions. Provided that you have more winners than losers, a ratio of three is excellent.

Right brain: The human brain is divided into two hemispheres, the left and right, each of which is responsible for specific functions in human behavior and existence. The right brain is considered to be primarily responsible for feelings, emotions and creativity. The right brain tends to think in pictures as opposed to words and is able to look at the big picture as opposed to minute detail. Those of us that are more creative tend to be considered "right brain thinkers."

Risk: The price of being wrong about an investment or trade.

Risk control: See *Money management.*

Russell 2000 Index: A capitalization-weighted index designed to track the performance of the 2,000 smallest United States stocks included in the Russell 3000 Index.

Russell 3000 Index: A capitalization-weighted index designed to track the performance of the 3,000 largest and most liquid United States stocks.

S&P 500 Composite Stock Price Index: A capitalization-weighted index designed to track the performance of the 500 stocks of the S&P 500. Stocks are included in the index based on their liquidity, market-cap, and sector. While not necessarily the 500 largest U.S. companies, these are generally the 500 most widely held.

S&P e-mini: Often abbreviated to "e-mini" and designated by the commodity ticker symbol ES, is a stock market index futures contract traded on the Chicago Mercantile Exchange's Globex® electronic trading platform.

Scaling in: Refers to adding onto your current trade position to increase your trade size. Scale in only if the trade or investment is already profitable.

Scaling out: Exiting 30 percent of your position when your trading rules tell you to. This is a technique that is effective in reducing stress and locking in profit.

Scalper: A trader who seeks to profit from very small price fluctuations. They buy and sell quickly to make a quick profit. They often use stop and reverse (SAR) techniques. They can trade larger trade sizes than trend traders and still maintain proper risk control.

Seasonal trading: Trading based upon consistent, predictable changes in price during the year due to production cycles or demand cycles.

Securities: Also known as stocks.

Securities and Exchange Commission (SEC): The federal agency that is designed to promote full public disclosure and protect the investing public against fraudulent practices in the securities markets.

Setup: When your trading rules identify certain criteria that must be present prior to entering the market.

Share: This is a unit of measure for financial instruments including stocks, mutual funds, limited partnerships, and real estate investment trusts (REITs). A person who owns a share is called a shareholder.

Short: When you sell before you have bought the item, you are "shorting" the market. This position is implemented with a sale, which profits from a declining price market. The term also refers to the trader or entity holding such a position.

Short call: When you sell a call option that you don't already own.

Short put: To sell a put option.

Sideways market: Also known as a bracketed, consolidating, channeled or non-trending market. See *Bracketed market.*

Slippage: The difference in price between what you expect to pay when you enter the market and what you actually pay. For example, if you attempt to buy at 20 and you end up buying at 20.5, you have a half point of slippage.

Small cap: Refers to the relative size of a firm's market capitalization. Traditionally, any firm with a market cap under $10 billion was referred to as small cap.

Speculator: A person who willingly accepts risk by buying and selling financial instruments or commodities in the hopes of profiting from anticipated price movements.

Split: The division of outstanding shares of a corporation into a larger or smaller number of shares. For example: In a 3-for-1 split, each holder of 100 shares before would now have 300 shares.

Spread: The difference between the bid price and the ask price.

Standard & Poor's Corporation (S&P): A company well known for its rating of stocks and bonds according to investment risk (the Standard & Poor's Rating) and for compiling the Standard & Poor's Index.

Stochastic: An overbought-oversold indicator, made popular by George Lane, which is based on the observation that prices close near the high of the day in an uptrend. In a downtrend they close near the low of the day.

Stock: A financial instrument that signifies an ownership position in a corporation. Stock is the capital raised by a corporation through the issuance of shares. A person that holds at least a partial share of stock is called a shareholder.

Stock symbol: A unique four- or five-letter symbol assigned to a Nasdaq security that is used for identifying it on stock tickers, in newspapers, on on-line services, and in automated information retrieval systems. If a fifth letter appears, it identifies the issue as other than a single issue of common or capital stock.

Stock market: This is a market for the trading and investing in company stock that is a security listed on a stock exchange.

Stop and reverse (SAR):   Used to close the current trade and open a new trade in the opposite direction.

Stop-limit order: An order that is triggered when the stop price is reached but can only be executed at the limit price.

Stop-loss exit: Also referred to as a stop, initial stop, or trailing stop. It is your designated price level where you have determined you must exit your trade if it goes against you. It is used to help control your trade risk. The worst-case scenario if the trade or investment goes against you. It is very important to determine the exit point before you enter the trade or investment.

Stop order: A buy order placed above the market (or sell order placed below the market) that becomes a market order when the specified price is reached.

Strike price: This is the fixed price of an option.

Supply = demand: When supply equals demand both the seller and buyer agree on price but disagree on value.

Support: In technical analysis, a price area at which a falling market is expected to encounter increased buying support sufficient to stall or reverse the decline.

Swing trading: Short-term trading approach designed to capture quick moves in the market.

Technical analysis: Price forecasting methods based on a study of price itself (and volume) as opposed to the underlying fundamental (such as economic) market factors. Technical analysis traders and investors use charts to detect patterns in the market. Technical analysis is often contrasted with fundamental analysis and some investors and traders use a combination of the two.

The Trader's Assistant: A complete trade posting and trade record-keeping system created by Bennett A. McDowell to streamline your trading and keep you organized by recording all trade information on "trade posting cards" and "trade ledgers."

The trader's mind-set: See *Psychology* for more information.

Tick: The increment of movement and price fluctuation up or down in the futures market is called a tick.

Ticker symbol: Standard abbreviation used to refer to a stock when placing orders or conducting research.

Time frame: The time frame is represented by a price bar interval time such as 2-minute chart, daily chart, etc.

Trade: When a buyer and seller agree on price but disagree on value a trade occurs. More simply stated, it is the point where the value of selling and the value of receiving are equal and the trade occurs.

Trade risk: The risk traders attempt to control through money management and risk control.

Trade size: This is also known as position size. It is the size of your trade or investment represented in the number of units (shares, contracts, etc.) of the market you are trading or investing in. Selecting optimal trade size is important in maintaining solid risk control.

Trade Size Calculator: Risk control software created by Bennett A. McDowell to determine a trader's maximum trade size based on certain variables such as percent risk and equity account size.

Trading: Opening a position in a financial market, either long or short, with the plan of closing it out at a substantial profit. If the trade goes against you. the plan is to cut losses quickly by using effective risk control.

Trailing stop: This stop-loss exit moves in the direction of a trend trade locking in profit in either a long or short trend.

Trend: The tendency of prices to move in a given general direction (up or down).

Trend channel: A trend line or series of trend lines used to identify upward- or downward-sloping trends by placing the trend lines on the highs and lows of the channel.

Trend exhaustion: When a trend ends it has reached trend exhaustion.

Trend trader: The trend trader trades or invests in the direction of the overall trend.

Trending day: A day that continued primarily in one trend direction, either up or down, from open to close.

True range: The true range is the greatest of the difference between the current high and the current low, or the difference between the current high and the previous close, or the difference between the current low and the previous close.

Ungrounded assessments: Trading and investing rules that try to forecast or predict the market. For example, MACD, stochastics, and Elliott Wave are ungrounded assessments.

Unrealized gain: The appreciation in value of an asset that has not been sold; paper gains.

Unrealized loss: The depreciation in value of an asset that has not been sold; paper loss.

Uptick rule: A stock market regulation that short sales can be implemented only at a price above the preceding transaction.

Uptrend: A general tendency for rising prices in a given market.

Volatility: Refers to the range of prices in a given time period. A highly volatile market has a large range in daily prices, whereas a low-volatility market has a small range of daily prices. This is a measure of price variability in a market. A volatile market is a market that is subject to wide price fluctuations.

Volume: The total number of shares or contracts traded during a given period.

Whipsaw: A price pattern characterized by repeated, abrupt reversals in trend. The term is often used to describe losses resulting from a choppy or trendless market.

Win ratio: Number of winning trades divided by total number of trades equals the win ratio percent (example: Win ratio of 60 percent winning trades).

About the Author

Bennett A. McDowell, founder of TradersCoach.com, began his financial career on Wall Street in 1984, and later became a registered securities broker and financial adviser for Prudential Securities and Morgan Stanley.

As a financial adviser, Bennett's niche was active trading and investing for a community of high-net-worth clients using his own proprietary trading system. This system later became known as the Applied Reality Trading, or the ART, system.

Bennett brought the ART software to the public in 2003. This was in answer to his clients' many requests for him to share with them his successful trading and investing techniques. Today, the ART system is used in over 40 countries around the world by sophisticated hedge fund managers and individual investors alike.

Considered an expert in technical analysis and complex trading platforms, Bennett lectures nationally and writes articles for many leading trading publications, including *Technical Analysis of Stocks & Commodities* magazine and *Traders World* magazine. Internationally recognized as a leader in trading education, he teaches trading to students worldwide through his company TradersCoach.com.

Bennett resides in San Diego, California, with his wife and two children and can be reached by e-mail via Team@TradersCoach.com.

Index